Home Improvement Projects for the Busy & Broke

Home Improvement Projects for the Busy & Broke

HOW TO GET YOUR $H!T TOGETHER AND LIVE LIKE AN ADULT

Christina Salway
Owner of ElevenTwoEleven Design

Foreword by Monica Pedersen

Skyhorse Publishing

Skyhorse Publishing books may be purchased in bulk at special discounts for sales promotion, corporate gifts, fund-raising, or educational purposes. Special editions can also be created to specifications. For details, contact the Special Sales Department, Skyhorse Publishing, 307 West 36th Street, 11th Floor, New York, NY 10018 or info@skyhorsepublishing.com.

Skyhorse® and Skyhorse Publishing® are registered trademarks of Skyhorse Publishing, Inc.®, a Delaware corporation.

Visit our website at www.skyhorsepublishing.com.

10 9 8 7 6 5 4 3 2 1

Library of Congress Cataloging-in-Publication Data is available on file.

Cover design by Jane Sheppard
Cover photo credit Christina Salway

Print ISBN: 978-1-5107-0589-0
Ebook ISBN: 978-1-5107-0590-6

Printed in China

Dedication

Holy shit, does it take a village!? They are not fucking kidding. The number of people who helped make this book possible is epic. The sheer number of hands involved was extraordinary. And I don't mean metaphorically, I mean *actual hands*.

I'd like to dedicate this book to all of the remarkable people who helped make it possible.

To my handy-dandy parents: Who taught me that I could do almost anything, especially if it involved home improvement. And for helping A LOT to make this book a reality.

To my husband, John: Who taught me that I can do even more if I Google it first. We are a real, live love story, plus a hammer. You are truly the best partner, collaborator, and co-conspirator. I thank my lucky stars every morning. Usually after I've had a cup of coffee.

To my son, Jules, and dog, William: You guys are aces too. Thank you for not minding too much when we didn't have a bathroom floor and for thinking it was funny when our kitchen cabinet doors were drying all over our apartment.

To our astoundingly supportive group of friends: Who all acted like it made sense that I was writing a home improvement book, even if I didn't think so.

To John's parents: For teaching us that we could write well and also be decent plumbers.

To my favorite under-thirty DIY enthusiast, Caitie: Because you're keeping us all alive.

To the dynamite team at Skyhorse: Who helped morph this book from stick-figure drawings into something that looks SO MUCH like a book!

But mostly, I should probably thank my mom: Because, seriously, she babysat a lot.

Contents

Foreword

When I think of Christina Salway, a couple of words come to mind: **Creative** and **Courageous**! I met Christina while working as a judge on a glossy, big budget, reality design competition show on NBC called *American Dream Builders*. After completing over three hundred makeovers on HGTV, I was thrilled to be on the other side of the table and given the chance to share with the contestants what I had learned from behind the scenes of designing for the masses. Oftentimes, this meant extremely tight budgets, nearly impossible production deadlines, sixteen-hour days, limited resources, and cameras rolling to capture it all—the good, the bad, the creative, and as reality TV often goes, the ugly. Luckily with *American Dream Builders*, I was behind the judges' table. As passionate as I am about design and as thick-skinned as I have had to become to work in front of a TV audience, I would never, ever, have had the courage that Christina showed to participate as a contestant.

On the first day of shooting, the producers allowed me to express in a few words what I wanted to see from the contestants. Naturally, as a do-it-yourselfer and self-taught designer, I said, "Don't be afraid to get your hands dirty!" While this seems like a simple expectation, for this group of designers, it was not. The contestants on the show were a handpicked mix of highly talented and successful professional designers. In their defense, if you have ever had the luxury to hire a designer you would know that you hire them for their experience, resources, and ability to execute their or your own design style depending on how apt you are. In other words, most professional designers do not do your painting, sewing, carpentry, cleaning out, and rearranging of furniture—unless your name happens to be Christina Salway. Of all the contestants, it was evident early on that she had these skills and mindset in her back pocket.

During the first week of touring the "afters" (TV talk for redesigned spaces), I was struck by the most beautiful children's room that was bursting with pattern, whimsical details, and an unexpected color palette (like all designers, I immediately took note to put this palette into my own designer file for inspiration). When I learned the room was designed by Christina, I quietly said to myself, "This is my kind of girl." Week after week of grueling—and I mean **GRUELING**—makeovers, Christina "brought it." Not only was she able to turn trash into treasure (I swear she could probably decorate your space out of an auto parts store), she always delivered spaces with the most beautiful mix of colors, pattern, and texture. And while the whole design world, including myself, seems to be designing in restrained neutrals, it was a treat to see the life and personality her creative design sensibility brought to each space.

On a personal level, her journey on the show was just as inspiring as her designs. I had heard early on from producers that Christina had moved her husband and eighteen-month-old from the East Coast to LA for the show. As a new mom myself with much doubt about going back to work and transplanting my husband, and seven-week-old baby, I felt both inspired and comforted that there was another mom on our set, with a shared passion.

No matter what challenges were thrown at her, week after week, Christina brought her courage, creativity, kindness, and down-to-earth design approach to one of the toughest design challenges one could face. I learned a lot from watching her, and if you have bought this book, you will too! Yep, I am a fan of this sweet, blonde, skinny-jeans-rocking design dynamo!

Happy Decorating and *Make It Beautiful!*

XO,
Monica Pedersen, *American Dream Builders,*
author of *Make It Beautiful: Designs and Ideas*
for Entertaining at Home

Introduction

All right. You've decided you're ready to live like a grown-up. This does not mean you have to stop getting embarrassingly drunk on Saturday nights, this does not mean you aren't allowed to spend your weekends watching Back-to-the-Future marathons for twelve straight hours, this does not mean you have to start making babies or decide what you want out of life. This only means that you are no longer going to live like an unemployed college student, surrounded by ironic *Onion* articles tacked to your walls and neon beer signs humming over your sofa (we'll talk about your disgusting sofa later).

It's time, guys. It's time to start living like an adult. Even if you aren't really one yet.

In this book, we're going to tackle some big and small projects that are going to make it a little bit easier to live like an adult. You're going to find some simple solutions to clean up your act—just a little —so that your apartment is actually a positive reflection on who you are as a person. To be clear: I'm not suggesting you throw everything away and make your home look like the IKEA version of the creepy murder apartment in *American Psycho*. Your home should not be anonymous. It does not need to be generic or barren. Your home should look like you live there. It should just be a representation of your best self, not your laziest, dirtiest self. Give it a shot.

And if nothing else, you'll be able to tell your aunt, or your mom, or whoever bought you this book that you did one of my projects and it's changed your life for the better. Win-win.

Rules of Thumb:
Harsh Words You Need to Hear

A Basic Guide to Living Like a Grown-Up

Living like a grown-up doesn't come easily to everyone. In the same way that you might have a friend who is just always immaculately dressed and perfectly accessorized, there are people with fashion style; people with an innate musical sensibility; people with an intuitive talent for cooking, and likewise, people who just know how to dress their home. Just because these things don't come naturally to you doesn't mean you shouldn't try. That's like resigning yourself to dressing in sweatsuits because you're not as fashionable as your friend. You might never compete on *Top Chef*, but if you practice enough, you might master a decent omelet. Don't quit—just do your best, consult the internet a lot, and when it doubt—the golden rule is always: put it away.

Yep. True story. The first rule to living like a grown up is PUT YOUR SHIT AWAY. And I'm serious. No more junk, no more clutter, no more "But I loved this beanie baby when I was in high school." I don't care.

Take a long hard look at your sentimental tchotchkes. Ask yourself these questions:

- Is there anything aesthetically redeeming about said tchotchke?
- Was it made before 1970, owned by someone interesting, designed by someone fascinating, or in some way unique that merits leaving it out for people to see?
- Does it serve any useful purpose? Does it hold something, hide something, allow you to sit on it?

If the answers to these questions is a resounding "No," it's gotta go. You don't have to throw it away, but it can't stay here. Put it in a Rubbermaid box and store it under your bed, mail it home to your parents, or do the right thing and donate it so some other sucker can have it clutter up their house.

GET IT OUT.

The second rule of thumb is the same as the first one. Now that you've put away all of your clutter and crap, apply the same theory to EVERYTHING ELSE in your home.

Put Your Shit Away

Hang up your clothes, you baby. Wash your dishes when you finish dinner. Put them away. Take out the recycling and put all that junk mail in it as you go. Seriously folks. When I visit people's homes, often times half of the problem is people literally aren't putting things away. When you get home after a long day of work, spend an additional two-and-a-half-freaking-seconds and put your shoes back in your closet. I mean really. I'm not trying to be a nag, but these are the basics. Your apartment will look and feel so much better if you just keep it organized. And I'm not saying you can't have a collection of beanie babies. But if that's what you're into, display them together, make them a collection—OWN THAT—don't have them scattered all around your apartment like some weird trapped-in-time-teenager-in-a-cat-lady's-body. Once you've put away all your extraneous crap, it will allow the things you've left out to actually shine. It's hard to tell that you love vintage fiesta-ware dishes if they're scattered all over your apartment with varying degrees of mold growing in them. How do I know that you collect antique medical equipment if you've got a twelve-inch glass syringe sitting on your kitchen counter and a broken stethoscope dangling out of your drawer, and between them, miles of dirty clothes and unopened mail? Once you put everything else away, you can start to make a conscious decision about what to leave out.

What I'm trying to explain is that everyone has their own version of what's awesome, and yours doesn't have to match mine. But if you apply these same rules to your weird collection that I've applied to mine, your home will start to look purposeful. Your collection will start to look purposeful. It will start to look like you chose to have your home this way, rather than it just happening to you due to a lack of resistance.

Make Your Bed

Shit. I'm starting to sound just like your mom. But seriously, the next step to living like a grown-up is also an investment in your own happiness. I don't just mean make your bed like pull the blanket up and put the pillows back on it. I mean *make* your bed. Make it beautiful. Make it purposeful. Make it a hotel-like oasis that you can return to at the end of a long day. Put a ton of fucking pillows on your bed so that when you walk past your bedroom, it calls to you. It says "Read a book here. Lie here for hours. Skip brunch and burrow into the peace and serenity you will find here." Yes. That is what I want your bed to say to you.

Start by buying some nice sheets. You do not have to spend a million dollars on sheets to have

nice sheets, but go buy a couple of sets of decent sheets. Go to your local discount home store and buy them. And when you do, open the zipper and feel the fabric. Does it feel like sandpaper? Does it feel like a creepy silky by-the-hour hotel sheet? Do not buy that. Your bed linens aren't meant to be funny and shouldn't be so cheap that they're crappy. They're meant to be soft, inviting, and comfortable.

And yes, I did say, "Buy a couple of sets." Because that's the next step to living like a grown up, and again—it's an investment in yourself. If you've got two or three sets of sheets, it means that you can rotate the various sets so they won't get worn out and faded as quickly, meaning that they'll last longer and you won't need to buy a new set of sheets for a longer time. It also means you can wash your sheets and have clean sheets on your bed at the same time. Yep. That's a thing. Maybe you haven't heard . . .

Now we get into the controversial stuff.

Duvet versus comforter: fight to the death.

First, let's clarify what these two things are, in case you're not familiar.

DUVET:

A white fluffy blanket that goes inside something called a duvet cover, which you're then able to remove and wash periodically.

COMFORTER:

A fluffy blanket that has a permanent cover, so in order to clean it, you wash the whole thing, or take it to the dry cleaners.

Assuming you sleep with a blanket at all, your preference for this was probably determined by how you were raised. As someone who was raised with a duvet and duvet cover, I find sleeping with a comforter kind of unpleasant. If I was going to be straight with you, I think it's a little gross. Because you can't remove the cover of a comforter, it tends to get washed a lot less frequently, and my mind ends up imagining gross seedy-hotel-esque conditions where I'm basically sleeping under a blanket of someone else's hair and skin particles. So yeah. In that scenario, comforters are pretty gross. If you think you're capable of routinely washing your comforter, or willing to take it to the dry cleaners to be washed every few weeks, this is the option for you. For the rest of us (slovenly, less prone to professional laundering services), the duvet is the way to go. In my ideal world, you'd also buy a few of these, so you can swap them out whenever you wash your sheets, but they're more expensive that regular sheets, so I'll understand if you only spring for two of them.

Now onto pillows: Maybe I should have explained earlier that I'm pretty serious about my bed. We spend a horrifying amount of time in our beds, and I really think it's one place where you shouldn't compromise. If you have cruddy pillows, change them. If you're not sleeping well, consider a new mattress. Spend the extra money. Get down pillows and a down comforter. I know that sounds bourgeois, which is pretty much unforgivable these days, but you're going to have to find it in your heart guys, because really, the difference is so pronounced. It's what separates the hotel-like-oasis we're trying to create and, well, a Motel 6.

My point here is that your bed should feel like a serene respite. It should always feel like an inviting, wonderful place to end the day, and part of that is making a beautiful bed in the morning so that when you get home—it's waiting for you that way. The pillows are in place. The blanket is pulled up. It looks clean and soft and peaceful. And that's the best way to end your day.

So for fuck's sake. Make your bed.

Honing Your Aesthetic

This one is a real doozy. It's not easy to explain exactly how one hones their aesthetic, but oftentimes I've found that who we are and what our home looks like go hand in hand. If you subscribe to that notion, your home is an extension of your identity. It's the space where you can display the many facets of your self—what you find beautiful, what you find soothing, what you find amusing, what you enjoy doing . . . The challenge is figuring out how you're going to incorporate those various "selves" without making your home feel like a chaotic clown-house. When I work on other peoples' homes, I tend to talk a lot about balance. What I usually try to find is the balance between the "calm spaces" and the "pop spaces." The idea is that your home should feel specific to you—it should feel like yours—but at the same time, it should be more like your online dating profile. It doesn't need to tell me everything all at once. Save some of the gorier details for the second date.

My point is, just because you love movies, doesn't mean your apartment needs to be plastered with the *Clockwork Orange* posters you had in college. Just because you love the color pink doesn't mean your apartment needs to be that color. I guess what I'm trying to say is that your home should be a tempered, more mellowed version of yourself. It doesn't need to be a literal, physical manifestation of all of your characteristics and preferences.

It's your sofa, not your soul.

Don't get me wrong, you also shouldn't be a stranger in your own home, and that's where the word "balance" comes back into play. Of course you want to be surrounded by things you love and enjoy. You just need to find a way to moderate those things so they don't take over your home completely.

There's kind of a formula to this balance that I like to use when I'm working with people on their spaces, and it's one that I've used in my own home as well. Basically, you have to figure out what's going to "talk." Talk might be a weird word to use, but what I mean is that each space should have elements that are silent, or subtle, and pieces that are vocal, or bold. Finding that balance creates a space that is harmonious without being boring, and exciting without being overwhelming.

For instance—if you've got a crazy rug, tone it down on the sofa. If you've got a zany sofa, maybe keep your wall color quiet. If you're really that crazy about pink, get a pink pillow. Frame your favorite *Clockwork Orange* poster and ditch the rest. In each room, you want places of peace and places of pizazz. That contrast will allow your brain to rest in between each element of visual interest so that you can actually see and appreciate those exciting embodiments of your personality, rather than getting so over-stimulated that's your brain basically says, "Yeah. I get it. You're kooky," and stops paying attention.

This is not an easy concept to understand, nor evidently is it all that easy to explain. It's absolutely something to be mastered over time, and honestly, I continue to "edit" my own house to this day. My recommendation: when in doubt, go with less. The less "assorted detritus" you've got in your home, the more outstanding those remaining pieces will feel. I think it's better to start with a more austere foundation and gradually fill in over time than to pile all of your shelves and surfaces with the memorabilia from every life experience you've had up until this moment.

The time has come. College is over. You're ready to start being selective.

Getting Motivated

How to go from Pinterest to reality.

This is going to seem harsh, but basically there's an underlying theme here in the first pages of this book. Have you realized it yet? At its simplest, the thing standing between you and your beautiful home—more than financial limitations, more than "not enough time," or "not enough space"—your primary obstacle is you. You have to make a commitment to your beautiful life. Think of it like a New Year's resolution. Like making an oath to go to the gym more frequently. Or to stop eating tater tots after midnight. Or to learn a new language.

Living in a more beautiful home takes only a little bit of your time. The time required to wash your dishes when you finish dinner. The time needed to make your bed and hang up your towels each morning. The time to put away your shoes and hang up your clothes. And make no mistake, I am guilty too. Six days out of seven (or maybe more like thirteen days out of fourteen) there is a growing pile of clothing "folded" but essentially heaped on my dresser. And then on the fourteenth day, I hang it all up and breathe a sigh of relief/pleasure

in seeing my bedroom how it's supposed to be—sans clothes pile. But here's the thing: it takes me roughly fourteen times longer to hang up fourteen days of clothes than it would if I just did it when I decided not to wear it the morning of. Like EVERYTHING else. If you actually hang your towels up and put away your bath mat, you won't have to devote your entire Sunday to doing laundry because your bath mat is filthy and your towels smell like bog water. (Refer to page 54 if you need some helpful hints on how to fold a bath towel nicely . . .) If you'd done your dishes when you finished dinner on Monday, you wouldn't find yourself spending three times longer chiseling dried, disgusting food off your plates on Thursday.

So it's not a lack of time.

And frankly, even a lack of money is a shitty excuse. Because although it would be nice if you could deck your bed out with piles of glorious pillows and luxurious bed linens if you don't have the money for that, don't. However, making your bed so it doesn't feel like a flop house costs you nothing. Same with hanging up your towels. That's free. And instantly transforms your home from careless to thoughtful. Priceless.

Not enough space for your idealized home? Another lousy excuse, honestly. All the more reason to take care of every square inch of your home. Even if you've got crappy, filthy roommates—make *your* bedroom an oasis. Hang your beautiful towels up IN your room, and tend to your personal space like it's a magical fucking garden. Because you might be broke and your roommate might be a slovenly bum, but by god, everyone needs respite from the day. Everyone deserves a haven, goddamnit!

This segues into the next question: How to get motivated? How to stop salivating over Pinterest and Apartment Therapy and really get in there. How do you make the change? In my experience, this is a snowball effect. That's why I emphasize starting with the little stuff (making your bed, putting your junk away, getting rid of your meaningless and dated memorabilia, hanging up your towels) because I genuinely believe that once you start seeing your home for its true potential, minus the piles and heaps and junk, you'll feel inspired to keep going, and really start improving.

That's why starting at *Martha Stewart Home* is pointless. Because it's like having an out-of-body experience to read about someone hand-making doilies in the shape of ducklings when you're surrounded by insurmountable piles of junk. You're like "Doily Ducklings? I can't even find my shoes! What am I going to do with a damn doily duckling!?"

But once your bed is made and your clothes are put away and you've washed the seven glasses that were next to your bed—maybe then you can look into your bedroom and realistically think, "You know. My bed would look a lot better with an upholstered headboard." And then I can teach you how to make that, and then, maybe you'll feel confident enough to try something new like that. Because look how far you've already come!

My advice: jump in (to the shallow end).

There's no easy way to get started other than just getting started, but it's good to begin with something simple. Don't break into your DIY lifestyle by attempting to build a treehouse for god sake. Start simple. Replace your bed linens. Buy a new shower curtain. Find a funky table on the street and follow the step-by-step instructions to spray painting it successfully. Start to feel the satisfaction and pleasure of making these smaller home improvements and that will embolden you to scale up a little. Remind yourself that you don't have to go from zero to master carpenter. By jumping into a smaller project, you'll also start to get more comfortable with the basics before you're confronted by some of the bigger challenges.

Diamond in the Rough

How to find a really good deal.

Here's the bad news: the world isn't what it used to be. For better or for worse. Just as our parents got to camp under Stonehenge when they were twenty, and run unsupervised for hours, riding bicycles alone until sunset when they were only ten years old . . . Those days are gone, and so too is the unbelievably good deal. Whether you blame *Pickers* or *Antiques Road Show*, the fact is everybody thinks they're "sellin' a gem" these days. In fact, 90 percent of the time, they think they're selling something more valuable than it actually is. Because as the old saying goes, "It's only worth what someone will pay for it." This isn't to say a good deal can't be found—it just requires a little more earnest hunting. But let's be honest, that's half the fun, so let's not tear our hair out about it.

My first hints

- Only buy the truly spectacular—or the exactly perfect—in an antique store (unless you're in a hurry or have a lot of expendable income.) When you shop in an antique store, you're also paying for all of that person's expenses: their rent, gas, the cost of the hotel room when they went to that flea market in Massachusetts. You aren't just paying for the thing. You're paying for everything.

- Scour garage sales and yard sales thoroughly. Head into someone's basement and garage when you're at estate sales. Dig through the boxes and baskets of junk! Often times the best deals are the pieces a person has forgotten they're selling, so don't just take a cursory glance and write it off. You're going to find much better prices at a yard sale than you'll ever find at a flea market, antique show, or shop—so it's worth the due diligence.

- There are a ton of terrific online resources, many of which require a bit of patience to really make them work for you. If you spent remotely as much time trolling Craigslist as you spend watching gifs of dancing cats, your home could be magazine worthy at this point.

Back to Craigslist, Chairish, Viyet, 1stdibs, and the rest of the online discount, second-hand, goldmine websites. There are two ways to troll these sites, and personally I recommend a two-pronged approach, though this may be both unconventional and a little boring. The first is obvious: figure out what you're looking for and put it into their search engine. Don't forget that not everyone knows as much as you about what you want, so don't just look for "Walnut Danish Modern Chair," for instance. Also try searching under "dark wood vintage chair" and "teak antique chair," and so on. And obviously, if you've got a specific maker in mind, search for that, though that's more likely to ensure that you find the thing you're looking for quickly rather than you get a good deal. Because let's be

Wait. Before I go any further, let's talk about that for a second. You're not going to like what I'm about to say here, but I'm just going to take the plunge. I challenge you to a test: Stop watching gifs, scrolling through Tumblr and Facebook, and diligently reading about Kardashian-related Hollywood dramas for a predetermined amount of time. Let's start with a weekend, and then maybe you can work up to a week or a month. Basically what I'm saying is put your phone down. Not "stop using your phone," because you know as well as I do that's simply impossible. I'm not saying stop texting or checking Instagram—I'm simply proposing a moratorium on "phone drivel"—the time you spend on your phone just occupying time . . . See how much you can get accomplished on your home, just by eliminating a little bit of the Internet from your life. I'm not saying become a well-appointed, beautiful-house-having hermit. I'm saying take a break from that stuff just long enough to get your living situation sorted out, and then you can return full time to snapchat and Instagram to show everyone how fucking amazing your apartment looks now.

honest—if you both know who Vladimir Kagan is—you're probably paying the going rate for Vladimir Kagan.

And don't underestimate using really simple search terms. I'm not kidding, try "chair." Some people just aren't as excited about mid-century furniture as you might be. Or maybe someone else thinks they're selling "tacky-Asian-take-out-chairs" and you think "bamboo = chinoiserie = Hollywood Glamor = A+."

There's a reason they say one man's trash is another man's treasure. They don't come up with these catch phrases if they don't apply!

All right. So that's the first part of our Two-Pronged approach to finding your perfect, unexpected, magically inexpensive gem.

Prong Two is the slow-but-steady approach. Basically, what I'm suggesting is that you re-focus your energy—the time you were previously devoting to Tumblr and Dumbledore gifs—and now spend a couple minutes each evening scrolling through the latest additions to Craigslist's "Antiques" page and the "New Features" on Viyet or Chairish. Literally, you can do this in about five minutes each evening, particularly if you do it frequently because then there won't be loads of new things to sift through, and it will make you first in line when someone posts that gorgeous dovetailed walnut mid-century coffee table as a "Brown Table for Sale: $25.00."

The perk of the second method is that you'll also inadvertently expose yourself to all the other stuff that is selling on these sites, which is actually a terrific way to educate yourself about what else is out there, who designed what, what's expensive, what's not . . . And you'll encounter all sorts of gems you didn't even know you needed. Which can be a blessing or a curse. But it's also a great way to end up with a stunning pair of retro bedside lamps when you think you're shopping for kitchen chairs. There is something lovely about this more serendipitous style of shopping online—it taps into a more intuitive, authentically curated style—so that you can find yourself excited by or intrigued by something not only for its practical qualities, but its aesthetic virtues as well. This spontaneous collection can also translate into a more organic ambiance in your home so it feels like a representation of YOU, not the folks over at West Elm.

How to Haggle, Bargain, and Make Friends

Okay, here's the secret to haggling: don't be a jerk. Actually, that might be the secret to life in general, which also happens to apply to haggling. Truly, the best way to get what you want out of life and flea market stalls alike, is to be a genuinely pleasant person: sincerely enthusiastic, polite, considerate, firm when necessary, clear about what you want and what you're willing to compromise. If you want to make an offer, don't offend them. Don't ever say, "I don't think it's worth that," unless you're willing to leave a sour taste in the other person's mouth. And remember, if you insult somebody, chances are equally good (maybe less than that) that they'll say, "Gee. You're right. That is a piece of junk. I'll take your five dollars gleefully." More likely they'll say, "Ya know what, buddy—expletive-expletive!" And then that guy is in a huff and you're no closer to the house of your dreams.

I recommend a more cunning approach, which will save everyone's feelings from getting hurt AND improve your chances of coming home with said object without rendering you penniless in the process. Try something like, "Ay!! That's really lovely. Such a neat piece. Eek. Above my budget though. This is a total shot in the dark, but would you consider _ instead?"

And they might say, "Fifteen dollars!? I couldn't possibly. But you know what, I could do twenty dollars." And then you say, "Hmm. I really love it, but . . . What about eighteen dollars?" And hopefully, if all goes well, you've just paid eighteen dollars for something that was twenty-five dollars, and everyone walks away happy. Obviously this is a totally hypothetical scenario, but the point is to politely whittle the price down rather than offer such a low number that they just tell you to bugger off. Also—and maybe this is just me—but people prefer to sell their old junk to those who are excited to take it. I think it goes without saying that it's nicer for the seller to think about someone else enjoying that thing they don't want than it is to feel like you got hoodwinked into giving it away. This might seem like stupid advice, but basically what I'm telling you to do whenever you're trying to haggle with somebody is to be your best person. Be charming. Be witty. Be likable. Is it so weird that I'm saying that? Essentially, I'm telling you to BE the person who should get a good deal. BE the person people want to see win. I swear it's the best way to get what you want out of any bargaining exchange, though

you might consider applying that concept to life in general. Just sayin' . . .

Next secret to haggling: nothing ventured, nothing gained. No kidding. If you really love something, just throw an offer out there. Send somebody an email on Craigslist and say, "Hey there. I've fallen utterly in love with your carousel unicorn, but it's totally out of my budget. I hope you won't be offended by my proposal—but felt I had to reach out to you, just in case. If you find that you've still got it months from now and you decide you just want it out of your hair, I would joyfully come and pick it up for $200, cash. Please keep my email address, and keep me in mind. Thank you!" Seriously. Because sometimes you do fall in love with a carousel unicorn and it is just out of your price range. But like I mentioned earlier—one man's treasure is another man's trash—a.k.a.: Just because that guy's horse is worth $5,000 doesn't mean he's ever going to get remotely near that on Craigslist. Every once in a while, someone would prefer to be done with it than hang onto it for years, hoping to get the right price.

So that's the gist. I wish I could tell you:
- Go to this specific store.
- Buy this specific thing.
- Look for these things at yard sales.
- You can buy this now and it will be worth more immediately.

But that's pretty ridiculous. I can't tell you where to find good deals in your town, but I can tell you how to get the best deals when you're shopping and the kinds of places you should be looking. The rest is up to you. Happy Hunting!

Striking a Balance

How to make your house not look like a DIY nightmare.

Once again, this is a matter of opinion. But I'm right.

Don't get me wrong, I understand the temptation. You're on Pinterest. You're scrolling through Apartment Therapy. You've discovered the truly limitless numbers of DIY websites and you feel inspired! Which is awesome! And you want to paint a chevron pattern on your old dresser! And you want to reupholster that chair you found on the street! And you want to put chalkboard paint on everything! And make ornate asymmetrical table arrangements and live with your dining room styled like there's a dinner party happening, with the queen, TONIGHT, every night. And! And! And!

Whoa. Slow down. Or don't, if you prefer, but your home will likely end up feeling more like an exploded test kitchen than a harmonious place to live. Personally, I think you've got to find some balance in the number of "wow" moments you have in your apartment, so that those wow moments actually stand out. Otherwise, people won't realize they are wow moments because they're being assaulted by the unending physical manifestation of all of the projects you've completed. Part of finding that balance, that harmony, is knowing when it's a good time to DIY and when it's just one pattern too many. Know when to put down the paint brush.

I think the best way to explain this theory is a series of do's and don't's diagrams, because trying to write out the hypothetical balance of the desirable amount of "zing" in a room is just more than I've got patience for.

In my book, what we're looking for is a balance of neutral and pop; manifesting in quantities large and small.

Example: bold sofa, quiet wall color, bold art work across from bold sofa. Mixture of quiet and bold print pillows.

Bold floor, quiet walls, bold art.

Quiet floor, bold walls, quiet furniture, bold art.

Maybe this is easiest if you think about everything in terms of "planes" in your apartment. The walls are a large "plane." The sofa is a large "plane." The floor coverings and floor are large planes. My apartment might be a fun example to analyze . . .

Our dining room and living room have zany painted floors—a deep beigey color coupled with a crisp white to make a wild, but not too wild, checkerboard floor. The walls pull from the white in the floor—a quiet "plane" in contrast with the "pop" of the painted floors. Then, there's a simple neutral sisal rug on the floor, which adds texture, ties into the color of the beige floor squares, and adds a little calm to the room. Sofa: quiet. Also beigey. Pillows: mixture of quiet and "wow," drawing from the other patterns, colors, and materials in the room to inform a balance of "wow" on an otherwise neutral piece.

This might sound a little milquetoast at first glance, but then POP! We've also got an 8' x 3' vintage candy store advertisement hanging on one wall! And look left, an IKAT-covered Eames chair. Hard to call that milquetoast. But the idea here is that those unexpected moments—

the things that make my space mine—shine because they're in contrast to a more serene backdrop. They say "Hey!" from one corner and "Hi!" from over there, rather than being a part of a visual assault, a cacophony of moments, all vying for your attention simultaneously. Because honestly, that gets exhausting. There's a lovely magic, a real art, in the silence between your moments. And it varies for everyone, but for me, I need a literal neutrality to break up my charisma. It's a little ying-to-the-yang, if I dare use that cliché without fully understanding its meaning. Like I said from the very beginning,

it's about finding a balance. A balance that works for you.

So, to circle back to the understandable desire to stencil your entire house, I'm hoping your newfound notion of balance can help steer (and maybe moderate) your temptations. Because it IS really fun to tackle these new projects, and you ARE allowed to continuously reinvent your home—so what you want to aim for is finding a harmony between your projects—find your aesthetic or tone, and let that influence your design. Maybe you installed a gorgeous brass vintage light fixture (using our directions on

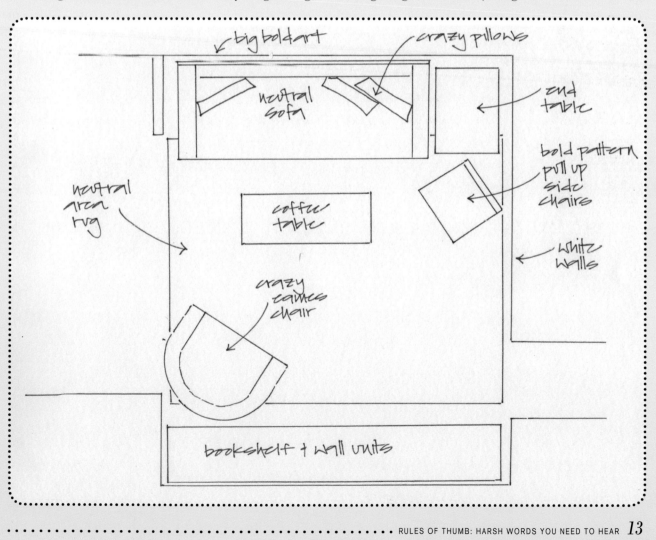

page 120) and you made beautiful pale green euro-shams for your bed (using the How to Make a Pillow tutorial from page 125) and now you're looking at that ugly old dresser that used to be in your Aunt Silvia's basement and you're trolling Pinterest and thinking that black-and-white chevron pattern would look awesome on that dresser. STOP. Let's evaluate. What's going on with your floor? What's your headboard made of? We've got green pillows, whatever your floor is, your wall color, your bed linens, your brass ceiling fixture, your bedside lamps. Whoa. We've got plenty of materials to draw from. I'm pretty sure there's no need to bring black-and-white into this equation, unless that's something that's already occurring somewhere else in your room. But that doesn't mean you can't paint Aunt Silvia's dresser with a chevron pattern. I'm just saying maybe black and white is overdoing it. What if we painted it with the same green as your euro-shams? Or even better—what if you paint it with gold-brass paint, to call back to your vintage light fixture? A brass and white chevron dresser would be awesome. And then maybe we paint your walls a variation on that euro-sham green? Get yourself a sisal rug for your floor, white bed linens and you're on fire!

All right, so you don't need to adhere to that ratio exactly—the point I'm trying to make is that some of these DIYs add sufficient pizazz to a room without adding unrelated colors, patterns, and textures to boot. Striking that harmonious balance can be the difference between "crafty" and "designed" and God knows we don't want our end result to look "crafty." That's like two steps from becoming a cat lady, and almost certainly the dating-world-kiss-of-death.

Do-It-Yourself Projects

(for the Average Renter or Amateur Homeowner)

Fast-Track Home Design

If you're not willing to read the whole book.

Okay. Some of you (not to stereotype, but I'm primarily referring to the men in the audience) might want to skip past all my witticisms and brilliant analogies and move directly to the end of each chapter when I give you the ASAP guide to home improvement. By that, I mean, "Shit. I forgot my parents are visiting this weekend and they're pretty curious about what I'm getting for $2,500 a month. With a forty-five-minute commute to work." Time to fast-track the charm of your apartment so your parents don't think you've taken up recycling as a form of income and drag your ass home.

1. CLEAN. How many times do I have to say this? CLEAN, CLEAN, CLEAN.
2. Fucking clean.
3. And while you're at it, consider doing a cursory tidying of your common hallways as well.

I don't know about your parents, but the first time mine visited my hovel in Brooklyn, they were almost as unimpressed by the state affairs outside of my apartment as they were inside. Graffitied front door, tumbleweed of dust and dead leaves (where do those even come from?), an ancient pile of grocery store pamphlets, and of course—the ubiquitous cigarette butts. My parents were underwhelmed, to say the least. And all I really needed to do in that scenario was sweep and it would have upped my residential clout significantly. Yes, eventually I also painted over the "meatface" tag on my front door, but you don't necessarily have to do everything at once. Don't overwhelm yourself or you'll end up quitting and joining the other slackers in your hall for a cigarette break.

Okay, your apartment is clean. This means you've swept, vacuumed, made your bed, folded your towels, taken out the trash, and hopefully thrown away all the molding, horrifying contents of your refrigerator.

Next . . .

Let's talk lighting and just how soon your unexpected/forgotten guests are arriving. If they're arriving tomorrow and your house is clean at this point, I'd recommend heading to your nearest home-goods store. Consider buying three throw pillows and four lamps (two pairs of matching lamps). Two of these pillows are going in your living room, two of these pillows are going on your sofa. Two of these lamps are going in your living room and two of these pillows are going on your sofa. The other two lamps and the remaining pillow are going in your bedroom.

Alternatively, let's say it's Sunday and your guests arrive on Friday. And let's say, for argument's sake, that you'd like to make a good impression . . .

1. Make sure you leave time for the pillow and lamp run, but let's aim a little higher!
2. The dimmer switch. I cannot emphasize enough the transformative qualities of the dimmer switch. Seriously. We're talking public housing to Park Avenue in less than

ten minutes. Don't skip this step! Consider Steps 1 and 2 essential measures taken toward long-term home occupation, peaceful relations with your parents, and (possibly, no promises) a vital step toward finding love. Because it's easier to love anyone in a pleasantly lit apartment, let's be honest. Installing a dimmer switch is an easy 1-2-3 project, and can probably be accomplished no matter how soon your guests are coming— depending on how easy it is for you to get to a hardware store.

Now we're moving into the extra-curricular/ extra-credit portion of our fast-track home improvement session. I'm assuming your apartment is still clean at this point, and you're still remembering to put your shit away. From now until your guests arrive, anytime you're home and you find your mind wandering—thinking "I should play a little Nintendo," or "I wonder if Joe's got any pot,"—first take tally of your apartment and make sure it's still clean and you're still putting your shit away. If that's the case, feel free to get high and play Nintendo until your parents show up. If not, get back to work!

3. Do you have a carpet? A basic carpet can go a long way. It doesn't need a pattern—in fact, rarely does it need a pattern—and it doesn't have to be wicked expensive to unify your living spaces. Consider picking up a cheap neutral rug for your living room (refer to page 87 to see roughly how large your rug

should be in relationship to your sofa, room, coffee table).

4. Let's replace some of the junky-generic light fixtures that are almost certainly in your apartment, and install something a little jazzier. Head to your local home improvement store and you should be able to pick up something a little more stylized for about $39.99. Worth every penny. Even if you can only afford to replace one fixture—choose the one in the most prominent location in your home and take the plunge. Follow the instructions on page 120, be sure you don't electrocute yourself, and voila! Instant charm.

In four simple steps (combined with a truly ferocious cleaning session), you've utterly changed your home. Obviously there's still more to do if you're planning on impressing anyone long-term, but at least this will keep the mice at bay, and comfort your parents while you actually get your shit together.

How to Paint Your Home Without Fear or Regret: Color Do's and Do Not's

The "choosing your colors" checklist.

I'd like to say that there are absolute rules about painting your home. Like "Never paint your bedroom green," or "Always paint your ceilings white," but the truth is there are always exceptions to the rules—daring individuals who paint every surface in their kitchen kelly green with stunning results; designers who love painting bathrooms black and ceilings gray; entire Pinterest pages devoted to red lacquered dining rooms. So not only is that inaccurate, but blanket statements like "Never blank-blank-blank" are stupid. However, I might put an asterisk in there that says, *"When in doubt, don't . . ." And that's what this chapter is all about.

When it comes to painting, the failure-to-success ratios are visible in first homes across the world, so if I can't show up in your living room to give you pointers firsthand, my best bet is to give you a reliable list of questions you can ask yourself and tips to guide your answers. The fact of the matter is that all I can tell you about the actual paint colors themselves is opinion-based, so we can agree to disagree on this one if you'd like.

My checklist tends to look a little like this . . .

Are you painting this yourself? And if yes, how good are you at painting?

"Why is this relevant when choosing wall color?" you might ask. Because certain colors are forgiving and certain colors are merciless. And if you suck at painting, you should probably stick to the easy ones, just to lessen your failure rate a little.

Dark, saturated colors are (obviously) more visible in contrast to your white ceiling and white trim. So if you're a miserable painter, the last thing you want to do is choose wall colors that are going to highlight every drip and error you make. At this point you're probably saying,

"But I was going to use painter's tape." Bullshit. Painter's tape won't save you. The thing people don't understand about painter's tape is that it *is not* intended for amateur painters to use, blasting helter-skelter around a room with no regard to trim and molding. It's intended to function as a shield when professional painters are cutting out a room. If you don't know how to do that, painter's tape will only lessen the leakage between your wall color and ceiling, but it isn't a guarantee. And it definitely isn't foolproof.

Honestly, in addition to giving you a false sense of security, painter's tape also comes with its own set of disadvantages. Aside from the frequent leakage/seepage problems, it also has a tendency to pull paint off of the surface it's meant to be protecting. And don't even get me started on the tedious process of actually getting it straight. If you think I swear a lot in this book, you should hear me putting up painter's tape (however, if you insist on using painter's tape, swing by page 23 where I walk you through the do's and don'ts of that nightmare).

So circling back, if you're not a gifted painter, you've got a couple of options:
1. Hire someone to do it.
2. Follow the instructions on how to cut out a room, which you'll find on page 23.
3. Choose a lighter, more forgiving color scheme, use a lot of painter's tape, and spend a fair amount of time going back afterward to touch up the paint with a teeny-tiny paint brush.

How much natural light comes into your home?

Paint colors vary enormously depending on the light conditions, so it's important to consider how the colors look in your home, not just in the paint store. I cannot emphasize enough how worthwhile it is to put a sizable sample on your wall before you commit to a whole gallon of paint. These days you can often request a custom color sample pot at any major hardware store—I know it's an extra five to ten dollars in paint, and I appreciate that you're trying to keep your overhead down—but this is an instance where being cheap doesn't pay.

BUY THE SAMPLE.

Paint an 18" x 18" square in a couple of different spaces in the room you're planning to paint. Look at it in the morning and again at night. Daylight versus artificial light change paint color dramatically, so you want to be sure that the "soothing gray" that you love in the morning doesn't look like "baby poop" by lamp light.

Does this color remind you of a holiday?

Easter is a BIG no—I pretty much avoid all saccharin pastels without exception. And yes, I still apply this rule when painting babies' bedrooms too. Call me dead inside if you must, but in my opinion, there are too many nuanced, beautiful shades of pink to excuse "cotton candy pink" in any application. Come on people! We can do better than that!

Other holidays you should be avoiding:

Weirdly, any time you put red and green in a room together, regardless of how NOT primary the shades are (we can be talking deep olive green and rusty coral) someone will say, "It kind of reminds me of Christmas. And not in a good way." It's the strangest thing. If you don't believe me, try it out. It's like the knee-jerk when the doctor hits you with a hammer. They just can't not say it. So unless that's something you're into, take Christmas into consideration when picking paint.

An oldie but a goodie: The Fourth of July. I know, right? I'm strict. Even if you own a house near a beach. For some reason, even though people can pick out Christmas colors from two hundred yards, time and again, they overlook the fact that they've dressed their house like a year-round homage to Betsy Ross and her glorious flag. And oddly, this is especially popular at the beach. For Pete's sake! Your home should not be a cliché. Just because it's close to the beach does not mean you should equip it like it's a nautical supply warehouse. Maybe make some rules for yourself when decorating a beach house:

- Strictly no red, white, and blue color schemes unless you plan to introduce a fourth color to that recognizable/overused trifecta.
- No flags of any kind unless you really are that patriotic.
- And for every one anchor or fishing net you install, you must have ten non-boating tchotchkes.

All right. You get my drift.

How do your colors look together?

This is really more of an opinion than a rule. I happen to think that the way each room relates to the next directly influences how you experience a home as a whole. I firmly believe in a cohesive, thoughtful aesthetic that flows fluidly from one room to the next. Not "matchy-matchy" (which is considered a fate-worse-than-death in interior design these days) but still a purposeful, considered design that has connections throughout the house. The first way to do this is obvious: literally, hold your paint chips together. Think about how they relate to one another. Does one of them jump out of the color scheme, seeming incongruous with the others? Here's a cheesy metaphor, but I'm going to go with it—think of your paint colors like musical instruments. Ideally, they all add up to a beautiful orchestra, the individual colors working together to create a cohesive whole for your home. If you throw a bagpipe into a classical concert, everyone's going to be like, "Whoa. I didn't see that coming." You have to decide if that's the way you want people to experience your home, and ask yourself, is this "unexpected-bad" or "unexpected-good"? Because they're not the same, people, they're really not.

Unless you're living in a studio apartment, the colors of one room directly relate to the colors of the next, and the way you experience them is in relation to each other. Even if you don't actually see them physically together, you remember the impact of one when you enter the next space.

Two rules in one:

- Just because a color looks good on you, doesn't mean you should paint a room that color.
- That said . . .
- If a color looks terrible on you, *definitely* do not paint a room that color.

Let me clarify this a little because it's admittedly confusing. There are all sorts of colors that look terrific with my complexion. Navy: awesome. Olive green: fantastic. But you know what looks particularly sensational? Coral. And all of the shades of coral. Rust, paprika, pomegranate. But especially lipstick-from-the-'90s coral. So that's nice. It's great to know what colors look good on you, and it will enable me to dress myself more like the cohesive, coordinated adult I pretend to be. However, it takes a really special gal (and probably an even rarer guy) to wake up to wall-to-wall coral every morning and not cry out in fear.

What's the take away here? Just because you like the color doesn't mean it's automatically suitable for an entire bedroom, let alone the recurring theme of a whole house. Don't take this the wrong way, but—leave the daring, nutty shit to professional designers. They paint people's houses like that because it photographs fabulously, not because it's pleasant to live in some loopy, lilac-on-lilac-on-lilac nightmare. They don't have to wake up there everyday, and half the time, their fancy-pants clients only sleep in those rooms a couple of times a year too, so it's not remotely as exhausting for them as it would be for the rest of us regular folk. Three hundred and sixty-five days of "daring" stops feeling daring at some point, and just feels fucking crazy. It's not "interesting" or "provocative" or "intriguing." For most of us, it just starts to feel oppressive, nothing more.

Which leads me to my next point, which sounds, at first glance, to be the opposite of my previous point. If a color looks terrible on you, seriously question if you want to paint a whole room that color. Even if you really like it. Because when you're having a dinner party or bringing home a date, you don't want your glorious, glowing face to be surrounded by a backdrop that makes you look like you've just been pulled out of a river. Obviously it's not the same as actually wearing that color (for instance, yellow genuinely makes me look like I'm a reanimated zombie, regardless of how much sleep I've had) but if you've painted your walls yellow, that color will still reflect a yellowish cast on you and everything else in the room.

*Disclaimer: At the rate we're going, it sounds like I'm basically just saying "Paint Your Apartment White," which more likely than not, your landlord has already done a half-assed job of. I'm not saying only paint it white. I'm simply saying don't paint it stupid colors on a whim. Your paint colors should add to the charm and design of your home. They should highlight its assets and distract from its shortcomings. It should reflect who you are in a subtle, appropriate-for-a house way, not just in a screaming-like-a-banshee way.

*But also don't underestimate the charm of white paint.

Wait. I've got another disclaimer.

Don't stress this too much.

After all that, there's one more thought to add to all of this: Don't take any of this too seriously. Take some risks too. Have a little fun. Don't cop out and just paint everything "linen white." In fact, unless you *really fucking love* linen white or somehow we've gone back in time and it's the 1990s and you're a New York intellectual living on the Upper West Side, never paint anything linen white. What I'm trying to say is that painting your house is not the same as tattooing your face. You can change your mind. You can have a change of heart. You can realize later that you're more conservative than you thought you were, and trade up for white after years of aqua. My point is that choosing your paint colors shouldn't stress you out so much that it paralyzes you from making a decision. Because, at the end of the day, you can always paint over it.

A note on colors: Just because you're a boy does not mean your color palette is limited exclusively to primary colors and colors that remind you of cigar bars. Not everything needs to be maroon or hunter green. You don't have to gravitate to different shades of chocolate brown in order to assert your masculinity. And for the love of God— black leather should be used sparingly. No one's going to think you're ladylike just because your sofa is beige, I promise.

Paint Like a Pro

I know we've already talked about my burning, semi-irrational hatred for the blue painter's tape, so let's not get me started again. We'll keep it short and sweet by saying that using blue tape motivated me to learn how to paint without it. That process is called "edging" and it's what separates the men from the boys. Or more like the pros from the amateurs. And once you've nailed this, you can pretty much use your paint brush like a pencil—you'll have such solid control over the way the paint comes off the brush.

There are really only two keys to painting like a professional.

1. Buying the right paint brush
2. Getting a lot of practice.

The paint brush I recommend most highly is Purdy's 2½" Angle Brush. Some of the contractors I know prefer the Purdy 2" Angle Brush (someone actually said to me, "Christina! What do you want with so much brush?") but you know what? To each their own. I stand by my 2½" angle brush. And don't overlook the brand. A shitty brush holds up like a shitty brush and paints like a shitty brush. Spend the extra five bucks and get a brush worth caring for, and it will be pay for itself over time, I swear.

Once you've got the right brush, it's time to understand how to use it.

I don't recommend starting with something you want to succeed at. Instead start by practicing on something you don't actually need to edge. Like, practice painting a perfect line between two vertical walls that will eventually be painted the same color, because if you fuck up, it won't actually matter and it won't make more work for you to fix.

Okay, here we go:
First off, dip your brush into the can a little over half way, to get paint on the bristles. Then using the side of the can, gently scrape paint off both sides of the brush, so that it is just lightly coated. Then dip the bristles back in a little less than half way and get paint on the opposite side of the brush from the edge you'll be painting. So for instance, if you were trying to edge between a wall and the ceiling, you want to gently scrape the paint off the side of the brush that will face the ceiling, so that the bulk of the paint stays on the side of the brush that will face down toward the wall. Then using the longest bristles (the pointiest part) think of that as your pencil tip.

Start at the corner, paint facing down toward the surface you want to get paint on, with the pointiest part in the corner, and pull the brush backwards, so the long point is pulling backwards away from the corner. Keep your eye on the pointy tip of the brush and keep it close to your edge and guide it along . . . Depending on how much paint you've left on the underside of your brush, you may notice it goes on heavily on the wall away from the edge. Once you've completed a nice straight line, you can return with your brush (without adding more paint) and hold the brush perpendicular to the edge to pull excess paint away from the edge and more evenly across the wall.

Holy cow. This is hard to explain.

The most important pieces of information are these:

- Use an angle brush.
- Get paint on one side of your brush and try to smooth off the excess paint on the other side.
- Think about the point of your angle brush like the point of a pencil, and use it to guide your straight line.
- Pull backwards on your paint brush to get the most control from your angled brush.
- Feather out excess paint once you've painted a section of straight line in order to prevent dried lumpy paint from forming.
- Practice a lot before you actually dive into painting. You can practice on an edge between two walls that are painted the same color (so you won't have to go back and forth trying to fix it) or even practice on a piece of cardboard and try to draw straight lines with the tip of your brush.

ceiling

once in position, use point of brush to guide paint...

wall

...and then pull brush backwards

majority of paint should be on the "wall side" of the brush.

this way...

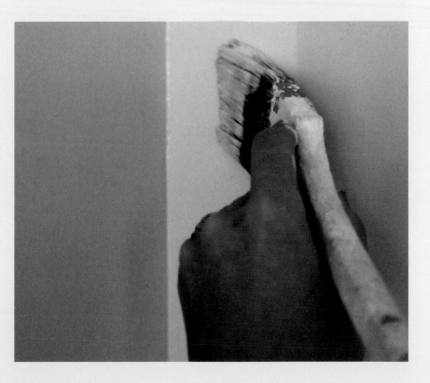

When you hold your paint brush, hold it the same way you hold a pencil. Really try to think about the tip of it and the way you use it just like a pencil. The real key to mastering the paint brush is thinking about it differently. It is no longer only a way to make big wide strokes, but also a way to make thin, precise strokes. I swear you can do this. Practice makes perfect. And once you've mastered it, not only will you be able to paint a room in a flash, but you'll never have to use that goddamn blue tape ever again!

Kitchens: On a Budget

Renovating your kitchen is pretty much the most transformative project you can tackle—but it's also one of the most expensive. If you're not in a position to go whole-hog, there are a bunch of "little fixes" which will drastically improve things without making yourself even more broke in the process.

You can consider these stop-gap solutions until you've saved up to do it properly, or you can square yourself with the reality that you're probably not going to gut-renovate this landlord-owned kitchen anytime soon, and make the most of it.

Replacing Your Kitchen Hardware Handles

This is an easy improvement that's basically a no-brainer. It's such an inexpensive tweak to your existing cabinets—a simple way to wash the stain of "generic contractor" from your kitchen without doing a major overhaul. And all it requires is a tape measure, a hardware store, a screwdriver, and a little patience screwing and unscrewing (wink, wink).

Let's get started: The first thing you want to do is measure your existing cabinet hardware. The easiest way to do this is to remove a handle and then measure the distance between the drilled holes in your cabinet doors. Refer to the little sketch below to be sure you're measuring the correct distance (this distance, FYI, is called center-to-center. The reason you need to know that is not to impress friends or potential mates, but because when you start shopping for new handles, the size of the handle is often referred to

as 3" cc, or 4" cc. This isn't the size of the whole handle, but the distance from the center of one hole to the center of the other. Center-to-center.).

Once you've determined that distance, double check that all of your cabinet hardware is the same size. You can eyeball it, or if you're not sure, measure all the handles so you know how many of each size you're going to need. Another thing to note: if your cabinets have visible hinges, you should consider buying cabinet hardware in the same finish as the visible hinges. This will make the whole thing look much more pro and much less schmo.

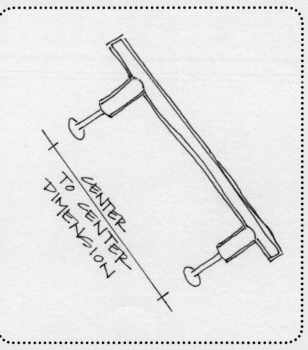

At this point, you can head to the hardware store to buy your new replacement handles. OR you can also shop for hardware online, where you'll find a much more expansive selection than what you'll find at Home Depot or Lowes. If you're doing your shopping in person, I highly recommend bringing your old handle with you, so you can double check your measurement and remind yourself what you're getting rid of. Another thing to note when you're still at the hardware store: you might discover your cabinets are too thin or too thick for the screws that accompany your new hardware. Oftentimes you can use the screws from your old hardware, but if not, you'll have to buy additional screws to accommodate your cabinet door size. Definitely ask for help at the hardware store if this feels daunting and someone can help you figure out what length will work.

Once you've got your new handles, you'll need that invaluable tool: patience. Because it's slow and boring removing and replacing cabinet hardware. The How-To for that is pretty self-explanatory: Using a screwdriver or drill (if you've got one) remove the screws from the back of your old cabinet hardware. Now, using the same screwdriver or drill, install your new handles. Dull, but worth every second, because in the end, your cabinets will have a new lease on life, and your kitchen will look that much less dismal!

How to Replace Your Kitchen Faucet (and Why)

This is another one of those projects that separates the boys from the men—or more specifically, the short-term tenants from the long-term. Because, let's be honest, if you're only going to live there for a year before you pack up for something better, you might as well not bother replacing the horrible light fixtures, painting the walls, or buying a gorgeous rug, and save the rest of your energy and budget for the next apartment. But, if you're planning to stick it out—these changes are worth every second and every penny.

Replacing your kitchen faucet is a great project to complete when you're in the midst of your other kitchen improvements, like changing the cabinet hardware, or painting the cabinet doors. It's a perfect opportunity to unify the aesthetic of your kitchen hardware—swapping out the grungy old faucet and dated drawer pulls for a more clean and contemporary style for everything. Head to your local hardware store—or better yet, IKEA—to pick up your new hardware. They have an awesome selection of modern handles and faucets, on the mega-cheap! The transformative affect of replacing this hardware will blow you away—it's like giving yourself a brand-new kitchen for about $150 total. When I put it that way, it's tempting to do it even if you are moving out in a year. Because 365 days of a nicer kitchen definitely has its perks.

So now that I've persuaded you to tackle this project, lemme tell you how:

Stuff you're going to need:
- Basin wrench
- Adjustable wrenches
- Putty knife
- A bucket
- New faucet
- Silicone caulk
- Plumber's tape

Start by picking your new faucet. As I mentioned, your best bet is to head to IKEA or a home store, and pick out a new faucet that will be compatible with your existing plumbing set up. If you look under your kitchen sink, you'll be able to see how many holes are in the sink, which will indicate the type of faucet you can buy. When you're choosing your faucet, also take note of how tall it is and how far it reaches into your sink. Different faucets are intended for different sinks, so don't overlook those dimensions while you're shopping, or you could end up with something wildly inappropriate for your kitchen.

Now you're ready to get to the real stuff . . .

Handy hint: I highly recommend sticking your head back under your sink and taking a photo of how everything is connected. You will thank me later when you're crammed in your sink cabinet, trying to figure out what connects to who.

Start by removing your old faucet:

- Turn off the water valves, usually located under your sink, and then briefly turn on the faucet to make sure all of the pressure has been released from the lines.

- Position your bucket under the supply connections, and then disconnect the supply lines from the faucet, using a wrench if needed.

- Now that it's disconnected from the water supply, you're going to physically remove the old jacked-up faucet from your sink. Using your basin wrench, loosen the nuts that are holding the faucet in place. Note: You may need an extra pair of hands to hold the faucet in position while you loosen the nut, or it will just go spinning around.

- Once you've removed the nuts, you should be able to remove the entire faucet. Clean off the grime left behind by the old sink, and scrape off any old silicone or caulk that might have been left behind. Be prepared—it will almost certainly be extremely gross under and around your old faucet.

And now we get to install the new faucet (This hasn't been too difficult so far, right? I told you this would be worth the hassle)!

- To install the new faucet, take it out of the packaging, and if there is a rubber ring or gasket that is meant to go between the faucet and the sink, set that in position. PLEASE read the instructions that come with your faucet carefully—not all faucets are identical, and you should make absolutely sure you're installing your faucet the way it is supposed to be installed—rather than ignoring their instructions in favor of my more general directions. I do not want to get a phone call saying your kitchen sink is leaking and it's all my fault, just because you chose to ignore a vital step to ensure successful installation. No dice.

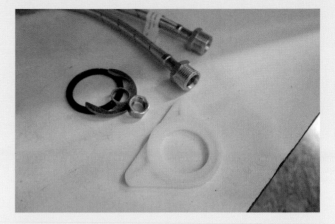

- Okay, now you're going to set your new faucet in place. Lead the water connection lines (connected to the bottom side of the faucet) through the hole in the sink, and back under the sink. Then, using your wrench, install the washers and nuts that come with the faucet, and tighten into position. You might need that extra set of hands for this part too—or again, your faucet may just wiggle around without getting much tighter. Now you're going to reconnect the water supply lines to the faucet hoses. I happen to be a big fan of plumber's tape (also called Teflon tape) which is used to get a nice secure seal when you're dealing with plumbing.

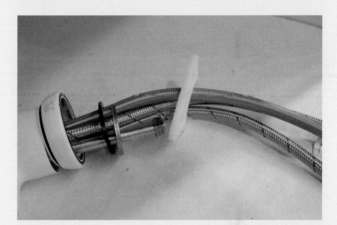

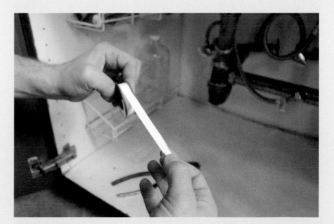

- You can wrap the Teflon tape around the faucet hose-end, and then turn the nut on the end of the supply line until it is tight. (While you want this to be tight, be careful not to twist this too-too hard or you can damage the threads on the hose . . .)

- Once you've reconnected both supply lines, put your bucket back under the joints, turn the handle so the sink is "on" and then gradually turn your valves back on. Watch for a minute or two to ensure you've got secure joints and absolutely no water is leaking out. If you're leak-free, you're good to go! Congratulations—you just installed your first faucet! See, I knew you could do it!

Revitalize Cabinets for an Instant Facelift

This is an awesome way to personalize your generic kitchen, but not for the average slacker. If you don't think you can keep your plates and glasses tidy, and you're not willing to make a plan and stick with it, hide your shame behind closed cabinet doors and go on your merry way. However, if you're game to make the minimal effort to keep your shelves and cupboards organized, and you've already taken the "drastic measure" to buy some matching dishes and plates, this is a super simple project that will really pump your kitchen up a notch. It's also a fun and inexpensive opportunity to incorporate one of your accent colors by painting the back of your cabinets with a punch of color; which will then allow you to buy inexpensive white dishes and plates to contrast with the brighter color behind. So if you've got the wherewithal, this project can be both a cost-effective and low-labor way to personalize your kitchen (without buying funny mugs.)

Quick and easy painting project:

More likely than not, the apartment or home you now live in has a kitchen. However, odds are good that aesthetically that kitchen leaves much to be desired. When I moved into my beloved hovel, the kitchen cabinets were warped, yellowed, grease-infused IKEA cabinets, begging for renewal. (Or replacement, if only my budget was bigger.) Since I knew I wasn't going to be replacing all of the cabinets anytime soon, I decided to opt for the quick-and-easy-budget-friendly alternative of . . . PAINTING THEM!

This is such an easy project with major results. You've got to put in a little time to do it correctly, but your skill level can be *really basic* and you'll get terrific results.

My plan here: Remove the upper cabinet doors, paint the back interior wall of the upper cabinets with a popping, eye-catching color, and then organize my dishes and glasses to create an open and playful display space that also provides ultra-functional storage in this urban kitchen.

There's only one catch—and this is what defines the amateurs from the pros, folks.

Doing this project only adds something great to your kitchen if you put things back where they belong. Yep. I said it. Put the glasses where the glasses go (shock!). Put the plates where the plates go (gasp!). Pick a spot for all of your plates, bowls, glasses, and mugs, and then *put everything in its place*. This is not rocket science. This is what separates us from animals with no thumbs. I know you can do it.

SUPPLIES:

- Quart self-priming matte or semi-gloss paint
- 2" Angled paint brush
- 4" Roller brush and handle
- Painter's tape as needed

STEP 1: Start by removing your upper cabinet doors. As you can see in this rental kitchen, the existing cabinet doors are discolored and old, and also have *dreadful* dated hardware, so rather than replacing the doors and handles, we're just taking them off altogether! (Don't forget: If you're a renter, your landlord may want those cabinet doors back one day, so find a stealthy place to stash them, like under your bed or sofa)

STEP 2: Take the time to prep your cabinets by wiping them down with a damp cloth to make sure you're painting on a clean surface. Then using painter's tape, tape off the area you're planning to paint, taping all fours sides of the cabinet that surround the rear inset. For this project, we're just doing the rear of the interior of the cabinet, so we get a bold definition against the colors of our dishware and lower cabinetry.

STEP 3: I chose a deep slate gray for my pop color, which ties in nicely with the dark gray countertops in my rental kitchen. I also have tons of brightly colored vintage dishes, so I didn't want to choose a color that clashed with or detracted from the vibrancy of my dishes. If you've got more neutral dishware to display, a bold color can enliven even the most ordinary sets of dishes! Using your 4" angle brush, begin by painting the four edges of each inset. (Note: Just because you've used painter's tape, it's still worthwhile to try to paint as tidily as possible, so that your clean up afterward is minimal)

STEP 4: Once you've finished all of your edging, come back in with your 4" paint roller brush and fill in the remaining gaps. Depending on the size of your cupboards, you may find a roller is unnecessary, but it will give you a more consistent, even coat of paint than a brush.

STEP 5: Once you've finished all of the painting, let everything dry for approximately 30–60 minutes (or until dry to the touch) before removing the painter's tape. *And then—the fun part!* It's time to style your dishware and platters to make the most of your transformed open cabinets!

*Be aware that the paint is delicate for up to twenty-four hours, so you might want to wait overnight before positioning all of your dishes and glasses.

Personalize Your Kitchen

This is a more labor intensive project than removing your upper cabinet doors and painting the recesses, but if you do it properly, it can really turn things around in your otherwise grim kitchen. About half the people I know in New York are living, against their will, with contractor grade semi-oak looking cabinets. You know the ones—raised panel. Reminiscent of a suburban basement in 1972. So ugly. So cheap. But it doesn't have to be that way. If you put in the time to paint your cabinets properly (and you maintain them thoughtfully), your landlord will thank you for transforming his miserable shithole into a magazine worthy home. And painting the cabinets is a great step in that direction.

I can't emphasize enough the importance of proper prep work for this project. Proper prep and proper paint will basically determine if this project works or ends up being a nightmarish disaster of epic proportion.

We're going to break this project into phases, because there are a fair number of steps, and you should really do this correctly or you AND your landlord are gonna regret it. Plan to devote at least a weekend to this project—not because it's forty-eight hours of work, but because there's a lot of drying time required between steps. So don't start this Friday night and plan on having people over for dinner on Saturday unless you're prepared to do your cooking surrounded by half painted cabinet doors.

Stuff you'll need:

- Fine-grit Sandpaper or sanding block
- Screwdriver/Drill
- Primer and paint, or paint with built-in primer
- Angled paint brush/mini 4" foam roller and Handle
- Blue tape
- Sponge and basic cleaning supplies
- Patience

Phase One: Getting ready

Start by removing all of your cabinet hardware. Take off each handle and each hinge, and label accordingly, so you know who goes where when it's time to reassemble.

STEP 1: Put blue painter's tape on the underside of your countertop to protect the counter from where you'll be painting your base cabinets. Likewise, if you're painting your upper cabinets too, put painter's tape on your backsplash, where it intersects with the upper cabinets.

STEP 2: Now remove the cabinet doors. Again, keep track of which door goes where—this will make it SO much easier to reassemble your kitchen when this project is finished. Do the same with the drawer fronts if they can be removed; if not, put blue tape around the edges to make sure you end up painting what you're supposed to paint, and leaving a clean edge around the rest. Don't be a slacker when it comes to using blue paint. The idea is that we want this to look professional, so sloppy edges are a no-go.

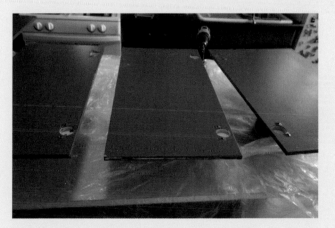

If your cabinets were really greasy or grubby, you might want to take this opportunity to spray them down with a household cleaner before you sand them. This might seem counterintuitive, considering you're just about to sand them, but in actual fact, grease will often smear and spread when you sand it, so it's much easier to get it off before you start.

Phase Two: Sanding

STEP 3: Once you've removed all of the hardware and doors, it's time to rough 'em up a little. Using your fine-grit sandpaper (or a fine-grit sanding block, which I happen to love) sand with the grain of your doors. If your doors don't have any grain (thank you, IKEA) just give them a gentle buffing to give the paint something to hold on to. The key here is gentle.

STEP 4: After you've done your light sanding, use a damp cloth to wipe everything down, so all the dust, etc. is removed before you start to paint.

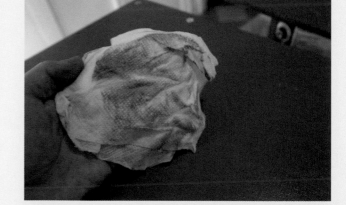

Prime Time (Sorry, couldn't not say it):
So the priming part of this project is mildly controversial. It's recommended that you use a primer first, apply to both sides, allowing each side to dry thoroughly (obviously), and then apply your paint after. But, if you ask pretty much any paint store guy (or me) they'll tell you that you can skip a step by using a self-priming paint and you get two-steps in one, which is hard to resist. I'm going to leave that decision to you, so you can't blame me later if you're not happy with your results. For your information, I'm really quite lazy (and you probably are too), so I opted for the self-primer when I completed this project, and as of this moment, I'm very pleased with my results.

STEP 5: For both priming and painting, you can use just an angled paint brush, or you can use an angled paint brush and a 4" foam roller. I happen to like the finish I get from a foam roller—it's about as close as you can get to a sprayed-on finish without having to spray paint your doors (which is basically an impossible undertaking if you live in an apartment. It's one thing to spray paint a chair on the street, but it takes a much bolder individual to lug a dozen cabinet doors out onto the curb to spray paint them. Not worth the effort or the scorn of your neighbors in my opinion.)

However, if you've got doors with lots of raised or recessed paneling, you're better off using an angled brush and skipping the roller altogether. And it's definitely easier to use a brush than a roller when you're painting the cabinet boxes and drawer surrounds, because you've got to keep a close eye on excess paint and drips. When you're applying paint, start with the backside of the doors, going against the grain of the cabinet, and then switching directions and going with the grain. This will get the paint thoroughly into the crevices of the wood, and get you a nice even finish. While you're waiting for the first side of the cabinet doors to dry, direct your attention to the cabinet boxes and drawer surrounds, and then when everything is appropriately dry, flip over and do the other side.

STEP 6: Now—if you've decided to use primer before you paint (overachiever) you will need to do another light sanding in between the primer coat and the coat of paint. Nothing vicious, just another light buffing with the fine-grit sanding block to give the next layer of paint something to adhere to.

If that's the case, don't forget to wipe everything down with a damp cloth again, and then apply your paint, first to the backside of the cabinet doors, then the cabinet boxes and drawer fronts, and finally, flip the cabinets over and paint the front sides once the backside has sufficiently dried.

Reassembly!

STEP 7: Now you get to see the fruits of your labor! Once you've allowed everything to dry really thoroughly (I recommend at least overnight, if not for a day or two, depending on the weather/altitude/etc.) you can reassemble your kitchen cabinets. Start by re-installing the handles and drawer pulls, before you put the pieces back on the cabinet boxes. The perk of doing that is that you can then use the handles to hold the cabinets while you're reinstalling them, which makes the whole process a little easier, and lessens the likelihood of you fucking up your doors before you even get to use them.

Then screw drawer faces back onto the drawer boxes, reattach hinges to the doors, and then (aren't you SO glad you labeled everything!?) reattach the hinges to the cabinet boxes. And there you have it, folks. You've just completely transformed your kitchen.

An important distinction: If you're priming and then painting, you can flip your primed doors over once the primer is dry to the touch. If you're using a self-priming paint, let them dry for a couple of hours to make sure you don't bugger up the paint when you flip them over.

Put your shit away.

I know I've already driven this home, but I think the kitchen is a space where this message can get muddled. In case I wasn't being totally clear, put your shit away. If I come in your house and find a counter top full of spices, bottles of oil and vinegars, and stacks of bowls and pitchers littering your surfaces—that's it. We're done. I'm breaking up with you. If I've told you once, I've told you a thousand times. Put Your Shit AWAY! I don't care how often you use that olive oil. I don't care if you use that measuring cup for your smoothies every morning. I don't care. It's no excuse. Use those wonderful appendages you've got (arms) and remove said measuring cup from the nearest drawer. Put your plates where the plates go (pick a spot in your cupboard and run with it) and just always put them back there. Decide where your coffee cups and glasses belong, and do the same. And you know what's great? If you just always put plates in one place and glasses in another, when you've got friends or guests over, they'll be able to put things back in their correct location because there's a clear location for each thing. Same goes for pantry goods. If all the canned food is in one place (not your counter!) it will be easy to see where it goes and where to find it. If all the cereal is in one place, that's where you'll keep your cereal. For the love of Pete, don't keep food on your counter, unless it's a beautiful bowl of fruit or vegetables. Google "kitchen design." Do any of those photos shown heaps of assorted dishware and piles of boxed food stacked up on the counter? NO! Because that's not the way to use your kitchen. It consumes your counter top space, makes cooking more frenetic and disorganized, and frankly, looks like shit. I'm glad you use your olive oil every day—it's a wonderful good fat and it's been said to prevent certain kinds of cancer. This does not mean you should leave it sitting out.

Okay. So you've decided to leave your olive oil out even though I told you not to. I understand that not everyone can fall in line—sometimes you just need to assert your own autonomy. Fine. Leave it on the counter. But if that's what you're going to insist on doing, do me (and yourself) a favor, and put it in a pretty bottle. Personally, I like to take an empty bottle of wine with sentimental value (from an anniversary dinner, a wonderful vacation, a lovely gift) and fill it with olive oil. Then I buy a bar pour-stopper, put that baby on top of the wine bottle and now you've got a bottle of olive oil worth displaying. And it's a little token of memorabilia to boot. Doesn't that look a little nicer than the shitty Goya bottle sitting next to your stove? Come on. Up your game a little.

Accessorize and Set the Table

And I don't just mean putting out plates and forks.

Setting the table seems to be simple enough—plates, forks, ideally knives since we're not heathens, and depending on what you're eating, maybe a spoon. Put napkins on the table and you're off to the races.

But let's step back and try to get this a little more "right" from the get-go, because there is a world of difference between a table set with mismatched, jacked-up plates and mugs of different sizes and the thoughtfully set table I'm talking about. This "thoughtfully set table" doesn't have to cost you a fortune—we're still aiming low here, so don't get nervous that I'm suggesting you set the table like you're a four-star restaurant—I'm just suggesting that a little cohesion can make all the difference.

Let's start with what to buy and where:

If we're really adhering to a tight budget: Head to IKEA or Target. You know I'm the first person to encourage secondhand or vintage purchases, but this is one instance where simpler is better, and basic white can't be beat. You can buy a complete dish set from IKEA for twenty-nine dollars, which will give you an utterly uneventful (but also entirely unoffensive!) set of dinner plates, salad plates, and bowls for six people. That's $1.66 per piece. Undeniably cheap. I'm not saying anyone is going to come into your house and say, "Wow. You've set a stunning dinner table" with a twenty-nine-dollar dish set from IKEA, but basically what you've done is applied the same "Clean it up. Put it away," home improvement theory to your dining room table. If you can't afford an arresting and purposeful array of strategically mixed-and-matched plateware, just err on the side of simplicity and your table and guests will thank you. And you will thank yourself, because even if you're only eating cereal in the morning, it feels so much better to start your day eating out of an actual bowl rather than that plastic chinese delivery container you rinsed out from last night. Because that's gross, guys. FYI.

Now let's apply the same logic for the rest of the table.

- Set of 6, or better yet, 8 water glasses.
- Same number of wine glasses. When in doubt, always buy extra glasses because:

A. They will break. It's inevitable.
B. You can never have too many glasses. Swear to god.

Set of six mugs. I really doubt you'll need eight. DON'T BUY MUGS WITH SAUCERS. You will never use them, and 90 percent of the time, mugs that come with saucers are actually teacups, which hold like 8 oz. of liquid rather than the typical 12 oz. coffee mug. It's a ridiculously small, completely unsatisfying amount of liquid. Don't be a sucker. Don't buy cups and saucers.

Please get rid of your funny mugs.

This will not be easy to do, especially if your significant other is the collector of these funny mugs. I still have funny mugs in my house after ten years of campaigning against them. If you win this battle, hats off to you.

Silverware: Once again, this doesn't have to be lavish. It doesn't need to be silver-plated, engraved, or antique. Just matching. Enough for everyone at your table to have a fork, a spoon, and a knife. So if you've got six or eight plate-sets,

get a similar amount of silverware. And just like glasses, you can never have too much matching silverware, so if you've got the option of a set of four or a set of eight, go with eight. Because at some point, you will accidentally throw a spoon away . . . Sod's law.

Napkins: There are various schools of thought on the napkin, and I don't want you to stress this too much. It would be nice if you'd buy paper napkins, so when you're entertaining you can offer your guests something a little nicer than a folded-up paper towel. Even if you only use these

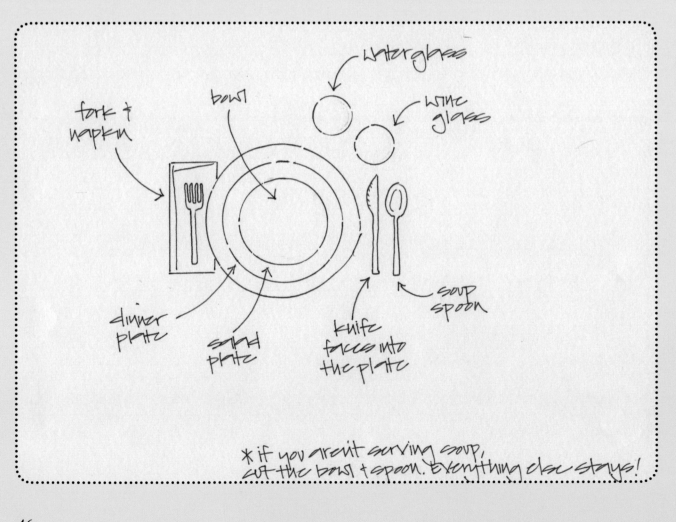

paper napkins when you have guests, splurge a little and keep them on hand. If you want to up your game a little, buy some cloth napkins. Again, nothing fancy. Please be sure they're machine washable and ideally, wrinkle-free. Something that won't drive you nuts, because if you buy something that requires ironing, you're going to curse the day you read this book, and me along with it. Personally, I actually prefer using cloth napkins so much that I bought a couple of sets for our everyday use; but if you're not feeling that fancy, you could just buy enough for special occasions (six or eight) and only break them out for guests. I think the napkin might be a defining moment in the journey toward not being a total fucking slob. Weird but true. When you decide you're ready for cloth napkins, it's like adding another badge in your "moderately grown up" sash. Because you're also saying "I'm capable of doing laundry regularly" as well as "I am willing to fold these pieces of fabric so they look nice." Those are both declarations that should not be taken lightly. You're really moving up in the world.

The point here is to simply and inexpensively unify the pieces on your table, so that your table

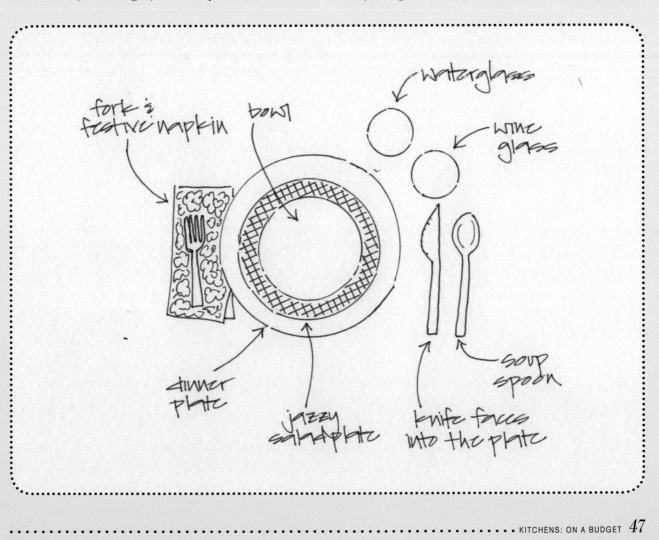

looks tidy. It may feel a little bland, but at least it doesn't feel like a dorm-room kitchen. And frankly, you can lay a table setting like this, throw a couple of white lilies into a vase, and claim to be a modernist. No one will even think you're being boring. They'll think you're being minimalist. And sophisticated. They'll never even suspect you're just being cheap.

If minimalism really isn't your style, and your budget has a little wiggle room in it . . . You can also add in a couple of fun contrast pieces to jazz this simple set up. Consider buying six contrasting salad plates so you can layer your plain and playful pieces together without making the whole thing look like anarchy.

Basic formula: White Plate/Bright Plate/White Bowl. And if you're ready to take the plunge: Colorful cloth napkins that speak to your colorful accent plates. Voila. Simple, with a little pizazz thrown in.

Still keep your coordinating wine glasses, water glasses, and silverware; and you've added some variety to your table without sacrificing the simple cohesion of our earlier place settings.

I know I sound like a hater here, but try to resist the temptation to lay your dining table like some overzealous Martha Stewart wannabe. All the gourds and tinsel make me uncomfortable, and will probably make your friends nervous too. When a table is so covered in crap, it's hard to know what to do with yourself or where to put anything. You get anxious that you're going to elbow over a wine glass or inappropriately disrupt (or accidently eat) the display—the whole thing is just too stressful in my opinion. Hosting a dinner for friends should feel welcoming and warm—not stuffy or contrived—so making everyone dance around decorative squash and orbs is down right unnecessary. Keep it simple: leave the mise-en-place to the Michelin-starred joints, the silly decorations to Martha, and just focus on being a good host. Because at the end of the day—it's more likely that your guests will remember if they had fun than they will remember your handmade name tags in the shape of ghosts. And frankly, if that's not the case: you really need to work on your social skills.

Bathrooms: Temple of Doom

Sprucing Up Your Bathroom

Let's start simple and eventually we can work our way up to some of the more ambitious bathroom renovation projects.

First: stop what you're doing and go into your bathroom. What do you see?

- Mildew-y tub, moldy tile work? ☑
- Rumpled, mismatched towels that smell like a dog bed? ☑
- Bathmat on the floor, dingy from being stepped on with shoes; damp from never being allowed to dry properly? ☑
- Hygiene products sitting on every available surface, often with the cap off and something oozing out? ☑
- Don't tell me: Is your shower curtain a picture of the New York City subway map? Does it have a witticism written on it, or have a funny cartoon of something? ☑☑☑
- Are your shower curtain rings those weird plastic circles from the 1980s that literally cannot be broken? ☑

It's time to step up your bathroom game, people. Part of living like an adult is not having a revolting cesspool for a bathroom. YOU ARE NOT IN THE DORMS ANYMORE. No one is going to show up and clean your communal bathroom once a week for free, so if you don't do it, it won't get done.

Let's start by taking down your overly charismatic shower curtain. This is a common misconception for some reason. I guess because bathrooms are hard to change without major renovation, people feel the desire to infuse their personality into the room by adding a funny or interesting shower curtain. Resist the temptation to do this. Really. I swear I'm not campaigning to make you all boring, milquetoast lemmings. I'm just trying to discourage you from having a bathroom better suited for a tween.

Because let's face facts guys, you're not tweens anymore. Tough luck.

So we'll start by taking down your personality-curtain, along with the dated plastic shower rings that probably came with your apartment. Then let's head to your local home-improvement store where we can pick up all of the supplies we're going to need to make your bathroom not gross.

> ### Here's what we're shopping for:
> - Heavy-duty vinyl or washable white cloth shower liner
> - Simple shower curtain (what we're looking for here is essentially white, with at most, a modicum of flourish. Maybe white with an eyelet pattern. Maybe white with a colorful embroidered trim. Maybe, maybe white and one panel of color, if we're really feeling adventurous. But even better: simple white linen. Oh yeah.
> - Soft Scrub Commercial Grade Cleaner
> - Depending on how grody your bathroom tile is, you might even want to spring for Commercial Tile Cleaner. "Zep" makes a diesel version that will spruce up even the most neglected tile work
> - Metal shower curtain rings. As simple as possible
> - Rubber gloves
> - Scrubby sponge

Now that we've got our supplies, let's get started. Basically, you're going to clean your bathroom. Yep. That's the gist of this "D-I-Y." Time to clean your bathroom and actually get it clean. If you don't subscribe to using toxic chemicals like Soft Scrub or Zep, I totally salute you. I just also have no intention of showering in your bathroom. Bathrooms should be clean. Really fucking clean. And for me, that means BLEACH. If you disagree, go hug a tree and we'll reconvene after I'm finished sterilizing this bathroom.

If I were you, I'd start from the top and work your way down. Put on your rubber gloves and spray down your tile work with the Zep (usually a diluted solution—read the instructions on the bottle). Let it sit as instructed, then begin washing it down, spraying the tile with your showerhead, scrubbing all the while and working your way down to the tub. You might need to do a couple of rounds of this, depending on how disgusting your tiles are, how much built-up mildew is on there and how discolored your grout is.

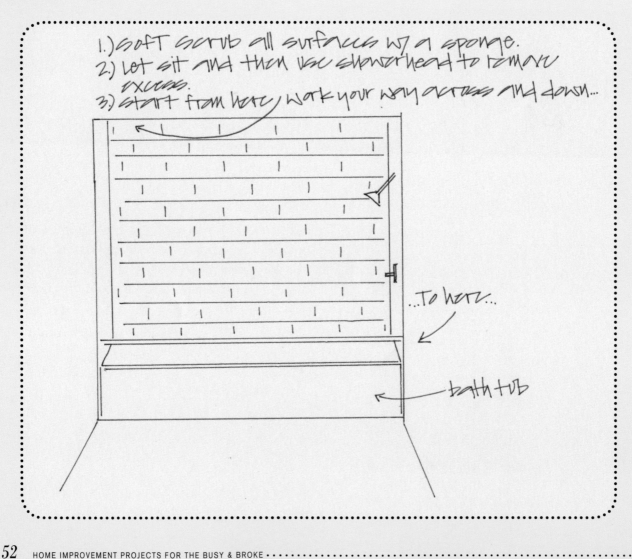

1.) Soft scrub all surfaces w/ a sponge.
2.) Let sit and then use showerhead to remove excess.
3.) Start from here, work your way across and down...

...To here...

bath tub

Once you've done that, tackle the tub. Bathtubs are funny—the grime there can be misleading. I've frequently found that I didn't realize the depth of the gross until I started to get the layers of soap scum and mildew off, at which point I was like, "Ooooh. So that's what a white bathtub actually looks like." That's where your Soft Scrub Commercial Cleaner comes in. To be clear, DO NOT GET SIDE TRACKED BY SOFT SCRUB ANYTHING ELSE. The "Bleach" version is nice or whatever, but it's amateur hour in comparison to the Commercial Cleaner. The commercial cleaner will get your shit next level clean.

I'd like to believe I don't need to explain to you how to clean your bath tub, but on the off chance this is your first time:

1. Put on your rubber gloves if you don't want old lady hands by the time you're thirty-five.
2. I recommend using your sponge to spread a thin layer of Soft Scrub over the entire surface of your tub
3. Allow Soft Scrub to sit for about 10–15 minutes for maximum effectiveness.
4. Turn on your showerhead and point the spray to the far end of the shower. Using your sponge, work from the far end toward the drain, wiping away the excess Soft Scrub and suds until your bath tub is completely clear of cleaner.
5. Use your showerhead again to direct the spray around your whole tub, to do a second rinse of everything.

Hopefully at this point your bathroom is already looking significantly improved. Now let's get your new shower curtain hung up. Put up your new shower rings, new shower liner, and finally—your gloriously understated, subtle new shower curtain.

Take a look around. Do you notice how clean your bathroom feels, just by changing your shower curtain and cleaning your bath tub? How it feels bright and airy, and moderately antiseptic. Kind of like an inviting surgical theater. That's what we're going for here.

Next steps:

Once you've finished cleaning your bathtub, apply the skills you've just learned to the rest of your bathroom. It's time to really get this room clean—like see-your-reflection-in-your-sink-faucet clean. You should hit your sink, toilet, floor, and any surfaces with the same aggressive cleaning ethos. Seriously clean your toilet. Soft scrub your sink. Use Windex or a similar glass cleaner to clean your faucet, shower faucet, bathroom mirror—it will make everything gleam in a way it hasn't since it left the factory. Once we've got everything clean, we can focus on the fun part: Buying some new towels, getting a bath mat, and figuring out how you're going to put your shit away so your toothpaste isn't leaking into your hairbrush.

Towels and a bathmat:

Do you remember what I said earlier about making your bed? I think I said something about the rewards of doing something in advance so that when you come back later, it's already done . . . Sound familiar? Well, the same deal applies in your bathroom. Essentially my message here is, "Don't be such a lazy slob." I mean really. Step it up a bit, guys. You're not six. You are fully capable of putting the cap back on your tooth paste and putting it into the medicine cabinet. You CAN find a place to put your toothbrush so it isn't just lingering on the edge of your sink, making everything wet and swampy. And you can definitely hang up your goddamn towels. I can't emphasize the benefits of this enough.

There have literally been studies done about the bacteria and mold that grows on towels in people's bathrooms—it's the perfect storm: it's damp, it's warm, it's sitting uninterrupted on your bathroom floor because you're gross. And before you know it—your towel smells like a wet dog and you do too.

So let's agree: you're going to hang your towels up.

Same deal with your bath mat. I know it costs you like an extra 5½ seconds to pick up your bathmat, but if you pick it up and hang it on the side of your bathtub or hang it up on a towel

1. Lay towel flat, the long-way, in front of you on a flat surface.

please note: towel depicted is NOT a beach towel with a cat on it.

2. Now fold into thirds, the long-way. First fold the left side 1/3 over. Then fold the right side 1/3 over.

over

3. Kind of think of it like wrapping a burrito.

Right side folded over left side

4. Now fold in half and hang over your towel bar.

* This lesson applies to hand towels, bath towels and even dish towels if you can see 'em.

rod or hook, it will have the opportunity to dry out properly that it simply won't have laying on your damp bathroom floor. It will also prevent it from being stepped on throughout the rest of the day, when you're not showering and are wearing shoes. All of this translates to needing to wash your towels and bathmats less frequently, and better yet—you'll need to replace them less often as well. And it cost you what? Maybe a total of twenty extra seconds each morning. Clearly worth it.

So the other thing I said about making your bed was that you should create your own personal notion of an oasis—something calming and soothing, a perfect place for respite each evening. Same deal with your bathroom. It should be a refreshing, spa-like experience when you go into your bathroom each morning. Invest in some pretty towels—ideally two to three sets of them as well as two matching bath mats. I don't know if you prefer your towels plush and fluffy, or those super simple, fast-drying Turkish joints, but decide what you like and then spend a little money to get a couple of sets. Make no mistake, you don't have to do this at Bloomingdale's in order to get something nice—I don't think I've ever bought a full-priced towel in my life. I strongly recommend hitting up HomeGoods, TJMaxx, or whatever the equivalent discount home store is in your neck of the woods, and finding something that works with the color scheme of your bathroom.

Lastly, how you're going to clean up the rest of your clutter:

While you're at TJMaxx, you can probably also pick up the remaining thing on your list: something to get you organized! Obviously this item is very bathroom dependent. Maybe you've got extra wall space and can hang up an additional storage cabinet or some shelves; maybe you're already at capacity, and the best you can do is put a little basket on your toilet, another one under your sink, and get yourself a little tooth brush holder. None of this stuff needs to be ultra fancy—the point is just to contain your clutter. It instantaneously makes everything seem more organized, even if you keep every last near-empty cosmetic tube that's currently making your bathroom a moderately gross nightmare—the very fact that it's contained in something makes it seem purposeful. It also gives you a tangible, literal place to put something away, which makes it so much easier to maintain a clean space.

So here's the take away, in order of impact and importance:

- Put your shit away!
- Hardcore clean your bathroom!
- Fold your towels or if you're really on a roll, buy some new towels!
- Change your shower curtain!

How to Replace Your Bathroom Hardware, How High Should You Hang a Towel Bar, and How Many Hooks Is *Too Many* Hooks?

There's a strong case to be made for replacing your existing bathroom hardware, particularly if you're in it for the long haul. Similar to changing the hardware on your kitchen cabinets, the miscellaneous hardware in your bathroom conveys a message of "accidental" or "purposeful," depending on what you've got. It's another fairly simple fix to improve the overall aesthetic of your bathroom, without doing a more expensive total overhaul. You'd be surprised how many bathrooms have a mixed-bag of hardware—a "contractor's special" of different finishes and different styles: polished nickel, stainless steel, a jacked up old faucet, a wobbly towel bar. It's like every person who lived there before you left their stamp: one person installed a new toilet roll holder, some other guy replaced the broken towel bar . . . And now your bathroom looks like a showroom for low quality bathroom supplies: one of everything, no two alike. Time for a facelift! Much like many of my How-To's, this project starts by removing the existing hardware to suss out how it's attached and what size you need when purchasing its replacement. Unscrew the towel bars, toilet roll holder, and if you're feeling really bold, consider replacing your faucet too. *IF YOU'RE GOING TO DO THIS, don't just unscrew your faucet. There are directions and steps for this!!

If you're going to replace your faucet, start by figuring out what style of faucet you already have, because you're going shopping for the same size fixture, in a more pleasing form.

Options are:

-Wide set: 3 holes required in your sink, with handles completely separate from the spout.
-Center set: This usually has 3 holes, but they're set closer together on the faucet. The faucet and handles are typically all mounted onto one unifying base.
-Single hole: One hole required in the sink, with the handle mounted onto the spout itself.
-Vessel faucet: This also installs into a single hole on the sink, but is typically a taller faucet, because the sink bowl sits on the vanity rather than in the vanity.

Once you've narrowed down the style you're removing, you'll be able to choose the one you want to replace it with. Before you remove your old one, go and buy your new one! The last thing you want is to be fooling around with this stuff, disconnect your old faucet, and then go get a faucet, leaving your roommates or yourself without a functioning sink until you've mastered the fickle art of indoor plumbing.

The obvious thing to do is to follow the instructions provided with the new faucet, but you might want to swing by page 31 to get a general sense of whether you're capable of doing such an ambitious project.

In the meantime, let's move onto replacing the other hardware in your bathroom. The idea here is to freshen things up, while also unifying the various hardware pieces so they all feel cut from the same cloth. Choosing pieces in all the same finish will instantly add cohesion to your bathroom. Aim for all the same style (or collection) and if you can't swing that, close cousins is preferable. With the exception of the faucet, installing these replacements should be a cinch. It's a basic "screw in, position, tighten" project—with major results. The difference between a five-dollar towel bar and a fifteen-dollar towel bar is night and day. The cheap one basically feels like stiff aluminum foil and the hollow towel bar will probably last you about eight months before someone manages to bend it; whereas the one that costs ten or fifteen dollars more actually has some weight to it—it looks and feels nicer when you're using it, and will actually hold up after years of use.

Follow the instructions on the packaging of each piece to see how to remove the old brackets and install the new ones. Typically this is a really simple swap-it-out process that won't require much more than a regular Phillips-head screwdriver and a tiny flat-head screwdriver (which is essential for installing bathroom hardware. Double check if the new towel bars and toilet roll holder that you're buying come with this tiny screwdriver, and if it doesn't, make sure you get one or you're up a creek. **Unless you've got an eyeglass repair kit at home, because that comes with the same little screwdriver. TMI? Maybe.

Installing a new towel bar is a little more of a challenge, but not insurmountable. You're going to need a proper drill, a tape measure, (ideally) a level, and your new towel bar. Using the template you'll find enclosed with your new towel bar, decide where you're going to position your new towel bar, measure from the floor and the ceiling to make sure both brackets will be level, and then mark where each bracket should be installed. Towel bars are usually installed 48" off the floor, or about 24" above a toilet, though if the positioning of your tile requires that you install it a little higher, it's not the end of the world. The template should show you the correct distance between each bracket—double check the measurement between the two once you've marked them to make sure you've got them in the right place. This is absolutely a situation where you should measure twice and drill once, because you don't want to biff this and leave a gapping hole visible once you're finished.

Once you've determined where the brackets are going, bust out your drill! Using the appropriate bit (it will say what size is best for the anchors provided with the towel bar), drill a hole for each anchor into your wall. Then position the first bracket, screw the screw through the bracket into the anchor, and then do the same with the second screw. Once both are in position, tighten both screws until the bracket is firmly in place on the wall. Then using your handy-dandy tiny screwdriver, tighten the tiny screw on the under side of the towel bar holder. Once you've done one side, you follow the same steps for the other side (install anchors, install bracket into anchors using screws.) After you've got the second bracket firmly screwed in, you'll have to do a little juggling—because you've got to insert one end of the towel bar into the towel bar holder you've already installed and then fit it into the remaining towel bar holder before you tighten the tiny screw on the remaining towel bar holder, attaching it to the remaining bracket. Did you get that?

This might be a little trial by error, but after a couple of fumbling attempts, you're bound to get the towel bar up . . . and then you can move onto the toilet roll holder. The steps for installing a toilet roll holder are virtually the same—place the brackets for the toilet roll holder approximately 26" off the floor, and about 10"–12" from the front of the toilet.

Can you have too many hooks? Probably. But if the option is leaving your towels on the floor, or having a ludicrous menagerie of hooks adorning every flat surface in your bathroom, I'd take too many hooks every time. That said, I'd rather you install one or two hooks on your bathroom door (be sure to use the appropriate anchors if you have hollow doors, or they will rip out after a week!) and then maybe one more hook installed on a wall near the shower, for easy towel access when you're showering. If you can keep your hook situation under three, it's better for all of us, and will hopefully discourage you from accumulating all of your dirty towels in your bathroom. Because that's gross, and you know it.

Make Your Shower Into the Spa You Deserve

I mean seriously! I feel like I spend a ridiculous amount of time in the shower (and don't even get me started on how much time I spend blow-drying my goddamn hair). And even though it feels like a profound waste of time, showering is also probably the thing keeping you employed, as well as making you a viable candidate for love and eventual pro-creation. So. If we've got to do it, the least we can do is enjoy it. And chances are, if you're reading this book, your home came with the ubiquitous cheap-renovation-lousy showerhead. Let's first take a moment to thank the shoddy contractors and slummy landlords of the world for cheaping out on this essential bathroom fixture—which we use every day. Cheers for that, buddy! And now, bitterness sufficiently vented, let's take our fate in our own hands and transform that leaky, junky excuse for a showerhead into something a little more rewarding. This is a profoundly easy project, and if you're showering as frequently as I am, it can truly change the way you start your day! There are tons of different showerheads to choose from—shop around online (be sure to read the reviews!) or you can even find a good one at your local hardware store. With a little bit of money and almost no time, you can have the spa-like shower you deserve.

Skills needed: Almost none.
Time needed: Very little.

Tools you'll need:

- Adjustable head wrench
- Marvelous new showerhead of your dreams!
- Plumber's tape (also known as Teflon tape)

*Some of you might not be the proud owners of an adjustable head wrench, and many of you may not want to become one either. If you're lucky enough to live in an apartment building with a super or a handyman (la-de-dah), I'll bet you ten dollars that they'll lend you an adjustable head wrench long enough to install your new showerhead. If you live in a full-blown house (la-de-dah)—which in my experience doesn't tend to come with a super—you should really consider buying an adjustable head wrench. Not only are they not very expensive (we're talking $4.99 here), but odds are good that you'll find another use for it during your time as a home-owner. If, like many of us under-forty-folk, you live in a miserable hovel run by a slumlord: a.) You're probably my neighbor, and b.) You more than anyone will definitely end up needing an adjustable head wrench again, so you should 100 percent take the plunge. When your kitchen plumbing is geyser-ing water all over your apartment floor and you're able to tighten the pipe and turn off the water valve, you'll sing the praises of your adjustable head wrench (and hopefully me).

Okay, enough rambling. Let's start with the obvious: Let's remove the existing crap-excuse for a showerhead. Use your brand new adjustable head wrench to get a firm grip on the nut that secures the showerhead onto the shower spout.

Turn the wrench counter-clockwise to loosen the nut, and once it's sufficiently loosened, remove the old showerhead.

*DON'T ACCIDENTLY BREAK THE SHOWER SPOUT OFF OF YOUR WALL BY USING TOO MUCH BRUTE FORCE.

Please, if you have a difficult time getting the nut to turn, do not go too kamikaze style on it or you risk bending or breaking your shower spout, which will make your landlord very angry. Consider using a little WD-40 to loosen up the seal on your old showerhead, so that you don't end up creating a much bigger project in pursuit of a very small project.

Assuming you've removed your showerhead without event: Use your fingernails or better yet, a razor blade to remove any leftover plumber's tape or gunk on the existing spout. You want the threads on your spout to be <u>completely</u> clean before you put your new plumber's tape on, to ensure a really tight connection when you put your new showerhead on. The good news is that if you

don't get it tight enough, you'll know immediately because water will start shooting out the side of the nut on your spout. Water shooting anywhere but down is not what a successful showerhead installation should look like. FYI.

Almost finished. Once the spout is completely clean, wrap a new layer of plumber's tape around the threads of the spout, starting at the opening and working your way back. Plumber's tape is funny, wispy stuff, but be sure you carefully wrap the threads of the entire shower spout to ensure you've got a well-sealed connection when you position your showerhead.

Put it on. Somehow this project description has made it seem like installing a new showerhead requires a degree of skill. This is not the case, and once you're doing it yourself, you'll discover how easy it is. Position your new showerhead onto the spout and "finger-tighten" the nut on your new showerhead as much as you can, turning toward the right. Then using your marvelous new adjustable head wrench, tighten the nut until you can't turn it any further and it's formed a tight seal on the shower spout. Ba-da-bing. You've got a terrific new showerhead that will offer you more than a pathetical dribble every morning. Congrats!

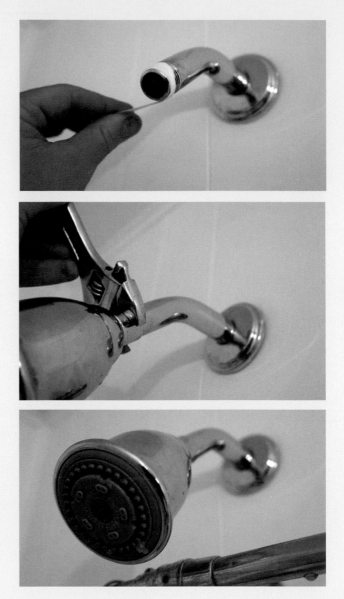

Not Fucking Around: Installing a New Tile Floor

Let me be crystal clear about installing a new tile floor: It is not for the undedicated. You should pretty much only tackle this project if you own your home and/or you REALLY REALLY hate your tile floor. It is a miserable task. Labor intensive, millions of steps, lots of opportunity for imperfection. Oh—that's the other thing. You probably shouldn't tackle this if you're a hardcore perfectionist because you'll get started and you'll never be able to finish. If that's you, blow the whistle now and call a professional. KNOW YOURSELF. If you are a perfectionist, please walk away now. Close the book here.

As I was saying . . . It is a miserable, time consuming, multi-stepped project from hell. Completing it made me feel schizophrenic— one minute I was like, "Why god, what the hell inspired me to do this again?" Because this isn't the first floor I've tiled and I'm confident it won't be my last. So while I'm hunched over on my bathroom floor, cutting tiny 1" tiles into tinier little slivers, I'm cursing every decision I've made in life leading up to this moment. And then two seconds later, I was like, "I am so proud of how great this looks. It's remarkable I know how to do this myself." And I was filled with accomplishment. And then I was like, "I can't believe how close my face is to the toilet seat right now," because I was cantilevered over the toilet, squeezing tiles into the tiny corner behind the toilet. My face was SO CLOSE to the toilet, I can still smell it. But if you're up for the emotional rollercoaster that is installing a new tile floor, let's get in there.

Time needed:
Basically three days, with large overnight breaks for dry time

Skills needed:
Medium. You do need to feel comfortable disconnecting and removing your sink and toilet, but the actual installation of the tile requires more endurance and patience than skill.

Tools you're going to need:
- Hammer
- Chisel
- Safety glasses (and if you're wimpy/wise, work gloves)
- Ready-to-mix thin-set (the cement that goes below the tile)
- Spackle knives (a couple different sizes will be handy. Maybe a wide one, like 4", and then a 2" and a 1" should do the trick.)
- BIG-ass bucket
- A couple of really big sponges. Think "car wash," not "wine glass" sponge.
- Spackle mixer
- Electric drill
- Grout float
- Level
- Compound nipper
- Notched trowel (There are different-sized notches for different-sized tiles. Look this up to make sure you buy the right-sized notched trowel. This is IMPORTANT. There is a right size.)

- Grout saw/sander
- Tile grout (I recommend sanded grout for floors, but I defer to your local hardware store guy if he disagrees. *But he's wrong.)
- De-hazing agent
- Grout sealer

- Tile! This is the fun part! When you're buying tile, make sure you buy ENOUGH. Length x width = the initial number. Then an extra 10 percent to make sure you've got enough, because you will break tiles and you WILL need extra. Don't cheap out. It will only spell another trip to the tile store if you cheap out here.

Let's talk for a second about what kind of tiles to buy and why: basically my argument consists of "buy small ceramic or porcelain tiles." Here's why:

1. You can cut them with a tile nipper rather than a wet saw, which is a MUCH larger, much more complicated, much messier tool.

2. They come on sheets so you don't have to separate each tile with spacers.

3. Because they're small, they are much more forgiving if your floor isn't perfectly level. If you use larger tiles, your thin-set layer really has to be PERFECT or your tiles will wobble on the uneven surface over time, and most likely crack eventually.

Prep work:

You're going to have to tackle the obvious shit first. You'll need to remove your existing sink and depending on your toilet situation, possibly remove your toilet as well. If you don't know how to do either of those things, but you feel handy and confident, look it up online and give it a go. MAKE SURE YOU TURN THE WATER OFF. If you feel doubtful and intimidated by the prospect of turning off your sink valves and removing your sink, it should probably serve as a LOUD SIGNAL to you that removing and installing a whole fucking bathroom floor is not the project for you.

STEP 1: So if you've got pre-existing tile that you need to remove, my apologies. Because removing tile in a space the size of a walk-in closet is a pain in the ass. And as far as I've been able to glean—there's no other way to do it than brute force, patience, and the willingness to hit yourself with a hammer a couple of times. (Just breathe through it, or have better aim than I do.)

STEP 2: Start by putting on your goggles and gloves. Then using the chisel, angle it into a grout-line at a 45 degree angle. Smack it hard, probably a couple of times, and you'll start to dig the chisel into the grout. Eventually you'll get that first mother-fucker up, and then you're in business. Make no mistake. This is hard. And will be for about 65 percent of the tiles. But every once in a while you'll get one of them up 1-2-3 and it will give you a false sense of hope which will fuel your willingness to continue. If you don't get those, try not to despair, even though 100 percent of your tiles suck to remove. I'm sorry your life sucks slightly more than mine did in this scenario, but just keep on plugging. I swear this is going to be awesome at the end!

STEP 3: You really want to be thorough here— everybody has to go! No stray little pieces of tile get to stick around, and no left over volcanoes of grout, which originally stood between two tiles. Out it comes! If there's a little bit of the old thin-set (cement looking stuff) which used to sit under your old tile left, that's okay, but you really want to aim high here and get as much up as possible.

If you aren't removing old tile before you install this new tile, bully for you, but if you're putting tile over an existing wood floor, you still have your own extra work to do, though it's SIGNIFICANTLY easier—you're going to want to install a sheet of 1/2″ cement backer board over your existing wood floor, which will reach from wall-to-wall throughout your bathroom. If this is your situation, it wouldn't be a terrible idea to google instructions for specifics, but the gist is "Cut cement board to size. Screw in place."

STEP 4: Okay, once you've prepped your subfloor (that's the fancy-pants professional term for the floor that goes under your tile) you're going to lay your thin set. Thin-set comes in a bag you buy at the hardware store. You'll need to mix the recommended amount of thin-set powder with the recommended amount of water, using your spackle mixer installed into your electric drill. Mix the thin-set until it's the consistency of creamy peanut butter. Consult a jar of creamy peanut butter if you need to refresh your memory on that consistency.

STEP 5: Then, using your trowel, and your spackle knife as needed, scoop about two cups of thin-set into the farthest corner, and smoothing it with your spackle knife, work your way out of the corner. Make sure you get tightly into the corner, using the spackle knife to squeeze it in there and wipe away the excess. You want to spread it so that it creates a nice even layer, the thickness is determined largely by how bumpy your subfloor ended up being. I am smoothing my thin-set into a 1/4″ thick layer and working my way out from there. The idea is to make this preliminary coat of thin-set as smooth as possible, so use your

wide spackle knife and/or the smooth edges of your trowel to make a nice level surface. Try to be pretty meticulous on this step, as it will absolutely impact your end results, but don't make yourself completely nuts, because there's going to be tile on top of it, so no one will know if it's not completely silky-smooth. Keep an eye on the time because if you dawdle too much, the thin-set will dry in your bucket and then you'll have to clean out your bucket, mix another batch, and start again. AND you'll end up messing up the stuff you've already done, which will be drying faster than the new stuff. Point being: Don't get so anal that you end up making a bigger mess. As you're working, use a damp paper towel to clean any stray thin-set off your tile walls. If you miss some, it's not the end of the world, but it's 100 percent easier to remove thin-set before it has dried than after.

IMPORTANT NOTE: Work your way out of the bathroom—starting at the far corner and making your way toward the door. Please do not thin-set yourself into your bath tub, or you'll have to sit there for twelve to twenty-four hours before it's fully cured.

STEP 6: Consult the instructions on your thin-set bag to determine how long you've got to wait for Step 2. Mine asks to dry overnight, so I finished my first layer, washed my tools in my kitchen sink, peed at my neighbor's house, and went to bed.

Okay, moving on. Now that your thin-set has dried, it may have cured to a lighter color of gray. According to my thin-set, that's what indicates that it has dried. Time to bust out the chisel and the level. Place your level to make sure your thin-set has created a (fairly) level surface, and then use your chisel to smooth out any huge ridges you have accidentally created as you were smoothing it out yesterday. If it's not perfect, it's okay with me—

BEFORE WE GO ANY FURTHER: Let me emphasize the importance of a game plan for this aspect of the project. You pretty much won't be able to use your bathroom for about three days while you're completing this project. I strongly encourage you to have a plan for that. Where will you shower? Where will you pee? Obviously you can brush your teeth in your kitchen, but there are some other things you really shouldn't do in your kitchen sink if you can absolutely avoid it. If you have a second bathroom, all I can say is "La-dee-dah." For the rest of us, PLAN AHEAD.

as long as it isn't like one of those topographical geography maps they used to have in grade school—but it is important to remove any of the more obvious mounds and moguls and fill in the more obvious craters. We have a saying in our house that may or may not bring you comfort in this process: "If it looked too perfect, it would look out of place." Granted that's partly because my whole apartment is a sloped, bent, parallelogram of a prewar tenement, but if you're replacing your own tile floor, I'm betting you're not living in a Hilton either. (If you are, even with my stellar instructions they're gonna be PISSED that you've decide to retile their bathroom, I can promise you that.)

STEP 7: So the thin-set is set. Next step: Vacuum thoroughly. Now it's time for a dry run. Lay out your tiles on your thin-set subfloor to see how you want them to be positioned; and then cut any of the pieces that need to be trimmed down to fit. I encourage you to do most of the cutting in advance, with the understanding that you'll almost certainly need to tweak them a little once you're actually putting them down. Now let's talk about trimming your tiles. First, let me be clear. If you've decided to use large tiles or something hard like marble or stone, you're on your own. My little tile nipper can't help you. However, if you're using a small ceramic tile (like I strongly suggested at the beginning of this undertaking) I can give you some hints:

1. Start by laying the tile down and using a pencil to mark where it needs to be trimmed. Don't just eyeball it. You can also mark multiple tiles at once, so that you can trim them all uniformly—and make a tidy little line.

2. DO NOT try to cut the tile in one chop. It won't end well. Instead, position the nipper about 1/4" onto the tile and squeeze. Please refer to the photograph to see what I'm describing. As someone who has installed more than one 1" hexagonal tile floor, I can assure you—there is a right way to do this and a wrong way. Both suck, but one ends with a pile of shattered tiles while the other ends in like an 80 percent success rate. (Believe it or not, I've consulted various contractors and pretty much across the board they agree those stats are the best you can hope for.)

3. Once you've chopped one side with the nipper (if the whole piece hasn't chopped off along your cut line, which happens delightfully frequently) reposition the nipper on the other side of the tile and repeat. And then- if need be- clip whatever remains in the middle.

To be clear, I'm not trying to make light of the thing. It's a major pain in the ass. It's so tedious. It's really so boring. And when for some reason, even though you've done everything exactly the same way, the tile shatters into a dozen un-usable pieces; it really makes you question your life choices. But at this point, there's no going back, so you're just going to have to soldier onward, knowing that I too have once hated this very same experience with the same burning anger you're feeling at that moment. That said, once you've laid everything out and cut the vast majority of the tiles, it's time to fix them in place, so let's move along.

Mix up another batch of thin-set. Follow the same instructions—mixing until you've created a batch the consistency of creamy peanut butter.

And now the step-by-step for the actual installing-the-tile process:

Lay thin-set: Repeat the steps you did to lay your first layer of thin-set. Using your trowel, and your spackle knife as needed, scoop about two cups of thin-set into the farthest corner, and smoothing it with your spackle knife, work your way out of the corner. Make sure you get tightly into the corner, using the spackle knife to squeeze it in there and wipe away the excess. Once again, you want to spread it so that it creates a nice even layer, the thickness of which will be determined by the style of tile you're using. For my tile (1" glossy hexagonal tiles) I am smoothing my thin-set into a 1/8" thick layer and working my way out from there, but this time you're going to want to work in much smaller sections than you did the first time because what you're doing is lifting up a couple of square feet of tile at a time, putting down the thin-set, and then putting the tile back down before you move onto the next section of thin-set.

Next, use the notched edge of your trowel to create even grooves and ridges through your thin-set. Do this by positioning your trowel at a 45 degree angle and then pulling it with uniform pressure through your thin-set. Personally, I kind of prefer the control I have by using the narrower edge of the notched trowel, but I'd bet you money most contractors use the wide side to get it done

expediently. Don't forget you're not going to see these grooves, so if they're not identical, no one will know. The grooves create a suction that eventually holds the tile in place, so you want to be thorough, but you don't have to be nuts.

Once you've laid a 12" x 36" section of thin-set, position the tiles in place. Start by laying the sheets where they're supposed to go, and then drop in the little slivers and half-tiles once you've situated the big sections. Now, use your grout float to "tamp down" the tile. "Tamp down" is contractor for "gently but firmly press." Don't push so hard that it squeezes all of the thin-set out from under the tiles, but press firmly enough that you see some thin-set squeeze between the tiles. Just a little. If you lay your first tiles and tamp them down and a huge amount of thin-set squeezes out between the tiles, you've either put down too much thin-set or you're pressing too hard. Ideally you want the thin-set to squeeze up so that half the thickness of the tile is submerged in thin-set and the other half is still visible.

At this point, you just complete and repeat, section after section, until you've tiled your way out of the bathroom again. Don't forget to wipe up areas of obvious excess with a damp sponge or paper towel, and if you get any on the adjacent tile walls, wipe that off too. Do this as you go rather than trying to clean it all up by dangling yourself from the doorway once all of the tile is installed.

Now you're going to have to wait overnight again, so rinse your tools off in your kitchen sink, pee at your neighbor's house, and go to bed.

By the time you wake up in the morning, your regular tiled bathroom floor should already be looking A LOT like a regular tiles bathroom floor. The thin-set will have dried (lighter than wet) and if you squint your eyes pretty hard, it's almost hard to tell there is no grout between the tiles. Don't take this opportunity to quit now. You need the grout to seal the joints between the tiles so water doesn't eat away at the thin-set and you don't slowly flood your downstairs' neighbor, so press ahead. We're almost finished!

Before you install the grout, take a quick look at the joints between the tiles. If there are areas where the thin-set has pressed up too high, use your little grout saw to sand it down enough that it's even with the rest of the joints, and do another round of vacuuming to suck up any dust, debris, etc. that's settled since last night.

Installing the grout: This is an easy step—much less time consuming and MUCH less irritating than installing the tile, and it's really the frosting on the cake.

You can buy either pre-mixed or ready-to-mix dry grout. Among contractors, the dry grout is considered preferable—you have more control over the consistency, a wide range of color choices, and it's less expensive. However, if you're at the end of your tether and want to buy pre-mixed grout, I won't judge you either. Either way, follow the instructions on the grout of your choosing, and prepare enough to complete half of your floor (unless you're really quick or have a small bathroom.) Using your grout float and maybe the smallest spackle knife, scoop a couple cups of grout onto the floor and then use the grout float to spread the grout over the tile and into the recesses between each tile. Pay attention to what you're doing here, because you really want this to be fairly even and consistent from one tile to the next.

Again, work in sections—about 18" x 18" at a time. Use a damp sponge (damp, not wet. So get it wet and then seriously ring it out) to wipe away excess grout, without wiping out the grout you've installed between the tiles. So, you're pulling it across the tile rather than pushing the sponge into or onto the tile. According to my group of polled contractors, they just use a couple of sponges, rinsing, ringing, and repeating from one section to the next, getting ALL surplus grout off the face of the tile. While that's nice for them, I found that to be wildly inefficient and extraordinarily irritating, so I instead did a couple passes with my giant sponges to get the majority of the grout off, and then came back with a damp heavy-duty paper towel to wipe the rest off clean. You still have to be very careful not to wipe away the grout between the tiles, but I found I got the remaining grout off a zillion times faster with paper towel than with the sponge.

*I also googled this technique and asked my favorite contractor about it. No one seems to be able to tell me why it shouldn't be done with a paper towel, so I don't know if this is a new-school vs. old-school thing, or what. Or maybe secretly everyone is using paper towel and not admitting it? My attitude: whatever I'm wasting in paper towel I'm saving in water by not rinsing out my sponges one million fricking times to get this done.

You repeat this same process in much the same way you have every other step. Section by section, working your way toward the door, cleaning up as you go. When you run out of your initial batch of grout, mix up another round and continue to work your way out the door. Once you're completely finished and you've thoroughly wiped the surplus grout from all of the tile joints, you have one more night of waiting. I'm sorry. I know that you're ready to pee in your own house. This is the last time you'll have to ask your neighbor, I promise. (And you should probably buy them a bottle of wine or a six-er of beer to thank them for the inconvenience, if I were you.)

The next morning your grout will be dry! You can use a de-hazing agent or a mixture of water and white vinegar to wipe any leftover grout residue (called "haze") from the tiles, and then apply a grout sealer to protect the grout over time. Follow the instructions on both of those products and proceed accordingly. My contractor said the best way to seal grout when you're using such little tiles is a roll-on applicator, but see what you can find at your local hardware store.

The final step: re-install your sink (or like we did, take this opportunity to replace your old sink with something nicer). In our case, our old, decaying sink vanity was literally being held together in places by the paint I'd applied, so it was time to go! I tracked down a brand-new fancy pants pedestal sink, complete with faucet on Craigslist, and bob's your uncle! In it went! If you had to remove your toilet, re-install. In our case, some bright star had cemented our toilet into many previous years of thin-set, so we had to tile up to our toilet base rather than tiling under

it. This isn't ideal, but it did allow us to pee in-house before starting the next step each morning, which was a little bonus.

The conclusion is this: I may be many (many) years away from being able to pay someone to tile my bathroom, but you know what, I did a pretty freaking good job myself, so to heck with that guy. And frankly, if I can do it, so can you. This is not a project requiring a great deal of skill. But it does require a truly extraordinary amount of patience and perseverance. But if the options are perseverance, parting with $2,500 to pay somebody else to do it, or continuing to live with the wretched tile I had—sign me up to tile another floor in a heart beat.

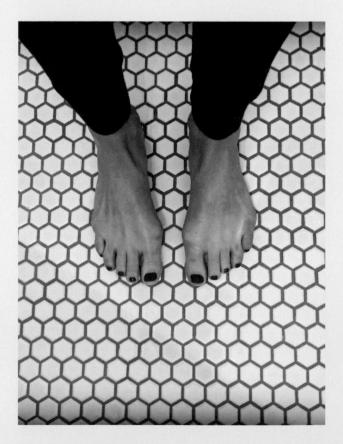

Fast-Track Bathroom Clean Up! Too Much to Do, Not Enough Time

I'm assuming we're dealing with one to two days advance notice in this "emergency home reno" scenario. So for now, let's skip stuff like, "How to re-tile your bathroom floor," (unless you're really motivated) and focus on the quick transformation stuff.

STEP 1: I know—I'm a broken record: Clean, clean, clean. And I mean CLEAN! If there's scum you can remove, REMOVE IT! If there's mildew you can bleach, BLEACH IT. The first step to not horrifying your parents, friends, and romantic interests is to show them that you're capable of basic human cleanliness. In the same way that you (ideally) shower and shave before you see your parents or meet a potential date. Basic cleaning goes a long way in the testimony of "I'm not disgusting" and/or "I am a moderately functional adult." After you've thoroughly cleaned your bathroom, everything else is icing on the cake.

STEP 2: If you're really broke, don't even worry about replacing your shower head at this point. If your shower curtain is a real atrocity, I'd make the case for a quick swap out. You can buy a white washable cloth shower liner for about fifteen dollars at any home improvement store, and even that is preferable to the slightly moldy, highly "dynamic" cartoon shower curtain you've currently got up. Eventually you can spring for a matching white linen/cotton shower curtain, but in the meantime, that white liner will look bright and clean, and will say loud and clear "I shower! I am not gross!" to your friends/family/possible future spouse.

If fifteen dollars isn't in the cards (remember—eating still trumps home improvement in my book) just take your shower curtain to the laundromat and WASH IT. If it's white or clear, wash it with detergent and bleach, and that should sort out your mold and gross problems. If it's got a stupid pattern on it because you just couldn't help yourself, wash it with color-safe bleach and consider having a heart-to-heart with yourself when you're in less of a rush about exactly why you think it's necessary to express your personality in the form of a shower curtain. Are you really that boring?

STEP 3: Sounds like Step 1, but isn't. Once you've cleaned your bathroom from top to bottom, you still need to get yourself marginally organized. Throw away the empty plastic holsters for your razors that are littering your sink surface. Put your toilet paper on the toilet roll holder. If someone you really respect is coming over, consider throwing out that revolting gob of soap sitting on the edge of your sink and invest TWO DOLLARS in a pump soap, for the love of Pete. And yes, hang up your towels and fold your bathmat. I know I've mentioned this before, but in case I'm not getting through to you, let me explain. YOUR BATH MAT IS NOT SUPPOSED TO BE A RUG. It is supposed to be a CLEAN PLACE for your CLEAN feet to dry off when you get out of the shower. It is not supposed to be a hairy, disgusting, dirt-caked piece of astroturf that's collecting every molecule from your bathroom floor. So please, please, fold it up!

That's it for the fast track to a halfway respectable bathroom. When you're ready, we can talk about installing additional towel bars and how high to install them; adding an extra medicine cabinet or shelf to accommodate your toiletries horror-show, currently overflowing onto every available surface; how to provide both flattering and functional lighting in the same room. But for now—you've made great strides in not disgusting your family and friends. Kudos!

The Easy Stuff: Your Living Room, Bedroom, and if You're Living Large, Your Dining Room

Your Sofa Is Ugly

Let's talk about your sofa. You know who you are. Your leather or faux-leather sectional—with reclining seats and a 42" seat depth—that used to be awesome in your parents' basement. I know. You love your sofa. And so do your friends. I don't care. You're an adult now and it's time to let it go. I know it's like watching TV while laying down, but if you want to do that, try your bed. Your living room is no place for that wretched, bulbous suburban relic, no matter how comfortable it is. It looks like a hideous landmass sitting in your home—and it's time to say good-bye. This doesn't mean you have to replace it with a wrought iron park bench. I'm not advocating for an unequivocally uncomfortable alternative. I'm advocating for compromise. For most people living in urban settings, your sofa is quite actually the LARGEST piece of furniture you own, so it would be nice if it didn't actively detract from the space and aesthetic of your home. This doesn't mean it has to be all form and no function—that would obviously be stupid. You still need to feel comfortable sitting in it, feel enthusiastic about binge watching episodic television on it, but it would be nice if when you're not watching TV, your friends could sit on your sofa and not feeling like they're being swallowed whole by a brown marshmallow from hell. So, with that in mind: Consider going with something a little more tailored.

How to Add Accent Colors to Your Home without without Turning the Whole Place into a Carnival

Mastering the accent color is the secret super power of interior designers—if you can find the delicate balance of adding accent colors to your space, you can make the most banal palette come alive.

Super secret tips:

1. Don't just choose one. If your home is predominately neutral and then there are just "pops" of purple or "splashes" of navy throughout, your space is still going to feel generic and bland, as well as overly matching and, to be frank, pretty contrived. Instead, choose something to pull from— is there a painting or a pillow fabric you love? Is there a set of colorful dishes you have on display that your accent colors can reference back to? Ideally, you'd start with your basically neutral palette, and then identify two or three colors you want to have reappearing throughout the space. And if I had my way, those colors would manifest throughout your home is different ways, so that you also get a pleasant, cohesive flow from one room to the next. And maybe that means eggplant throw pillow in the living room, eggplant vase in the kitchen, eggplant coverlet on your bed. But that can't be it. Otherwise suddenly your home is going to feel like a weird beige and purple zebra skin. If I had my way, you'd also have a glassy green pillow on the sofa, pale glassy green walls in the bedroom, and maybe a painting or fabric pattern/print somewhere that calls back to all of these colors. Hopefully you're getting my drift here—the idea is one I've touched on already—it's all about balance. Identifying a couple of colors you like in combination, and then figuring out how to apply different quantities of each so they feel pleasantly distributed throughout your space, without feeling overwhelming or overdone.

2. For your own sake, put your accent color on things you can change. This is also one of the greatest benefits of keeping your palette more neutral and understated. It allows you to swap out your accent colors if you get tired of them, without having to buy a new sofa or repaint your entire apartment. And if you start feeling really ambitious, you can swap out your accent colors based on the seasons. (Okay, maybe that's a little more Martha Stewart than we are at this point . . .)

3. Pick your accent colors based on how they look collectively, not just based on your preference for the individual colors. Red and green: Christmas- no matter how hard you try. Red and blue: Nautical, unless you've really got a gift with neutral tones to mellow them out. Think about unexpected colors too- rusty oranges, slatey blues, varying shades of yellow or green . . . Your accent colors don't have to be primary colors in order to be effective.

4. If you feel strongly about having an accent wall, I won't fight you on it, but I won't advocate for it either. The application of the accent wall is a tricky thing—you really need just the right spot for it, or it will just end up feeling like 2009 in there, so give real consideration to your permanent accent colors. Caribbean blue feels like a better idea when you're twenty-five than when you're twenty-eight, let me tell you!

5. Once you've chosen your accent colors, don't think this means you can only use those colors. Your accent colors are meant to be recurring colors that keep popping up throughout your home. It doesn't mean they have a strict monopoly on color— you're allowed to (and I encourage you) to add a little diversity to your palette with unexpected splashes. Don't not buy a vase you love because it isn't purple and your primary accent color is purple. And DEFINITELY don't buy a vase or painting you don't like, just because it is purple. As important as "balanced manifestations of accent colors is" (laugh as needed) it's more important your home feels collected and authentic, so please, please don't fill your home with meaningless purple tchotchkes, just because they're purple.

6. Consider painting a piece of furniture a bold color. Breaking away from the wood-on-wood palette of most casegoods can be a terrific way to add a little pizazz to your home. Take one of your more weathered pieces, and following the How-To Instructions on page 80, give that piece of furniture a major facelift.

A bold or bright color can be a perfect way to add a little POP in an unexpected way. The only downside to this—pillows are way easier to switch out than dresser colors, so if you decide to take the plunge, come to terms with the possibility that you might want to repaint it again a few years from now.

> Word of advice: Painting furniture should be done in moderation and installed with consideration. Putting one jacked-up spray painted piece of furniture next to another differently spray painted piece fools no one (okay, maybe a few idiots.) It just makes everything look like an arts and crafts project gone amuck, so if you're going to boldly spray paint a piece, make sure you've considered how that color will interact with the rest of the furniture in your space.

Street Finds: How to Revitalize and Reupholster Mix-and-Match Dining Chairs

Spray painting furniture is the fastest way to revitalize an old piece, and is also the perfect way to make a bunch of mismatched pieces coordinate! Mastering the art of basic upholstery means you've mastered the skills to make a junkity looking street-find into a real jewel, but more than that—by getting comfortable with spray painting and upholstery, the sky's the limit! There are so few street-finds or thrift store scores that can't be transformed with a coat of paint and/ or a cute piece of fabric; so if you're living on a tight budget—this is worth getting good at. And don't forget—there's a reason they say "Practice makes perfect." It might take a couple of attempts at upholstery to really get the hang of it, but once you've got it nailed, there's nothing you can't recover.

Skills you'll need: Very few!

Time you'll need: Very little! 30 minutes, max, plus a little extra for dry time.

Tools you'll need:

- Old chairs in need of a facelift. I highly recommend hunting in your family basement, at yard sales, or even on the street for the perfect candidate!
- Spray paint in the color of your choosing. (Estimate 1½ cans of spray paint, per small chair) I'd like to discourage you from spraying all of your chairs lime green, but never say "Never." Maybe that would be awesome?
- Fine-grit sandpaper or a sanding block (optional)
- Damp paper towel
- Drop cloth
- Staple gun and staples
- Fabric (quantities depend on the size of the seat you're reupholstering)
- Screwdriver
- Pinking sheers or sharp scissors (If you've got long-term DIY aspirations, you might as well spring for pinking sheers now. They'll come in handy a million times in the future, are delightfully sharp, and will keep all of your sewing projects from fraying into a sorry heap. Worth the expense if you're in it to win it.)

Prep work: Start by removing the seat from each of your chairs. Flip each chair over, and using your brain, figure out how the seat cushion is attached to the chair base. Typically, you use a screwdriver to remove the screws that are attaching the seat cushion to the frame of the chair. Set aside the seat cushion and take a second to put the screws somewhere memorable so you don't lose them. I highly recommend putting them in a little jar or cup so they don't sneakily roll away, but it's dealer's choice on that one.

More prep work: I'd like to say that depending on the finish of your chair, you could lightly sand the frame of the chair to make sure the paint adhers well to the surface, but the fact is you *really should* give it a light sanding, particuarly if there is an existing high-gloss or lacquered finish. This is going to take an extra 5 minutes, tops, and is well-worth the miniscule extra effort if it means that your paint stays where you want it to for as long as you want it to. Once you've lightly sanded your chair frame using your fine-grit sandpaper or a sanding block, grab a damp paper towel to wipe down the entire frame of your chairs. Spray paint is decidedly unforgiving when it comes to dust and grime—I swear it gobs up and highlights every freaking dust particle—so it's worth it to do a thorough wipe down before you start the spray-painting portion of this project. Sadly, this project is like oh-so-many home improvement projects— planning ahead and doing the necessary prep work will define your overall success—so put in the time now to ensure awesome results after. Boo-hoo, I know.

Now—get in there: Once you've removed your seat and thoroughly wiped down your chair, you're ready to spray paint! Position your chair on a drop cloth in a well-ventilated area—**otherwise known as OUTSIDE**—and make sure you have your painting station set up away from anything you don't want sprayed. Spray paint has an uncanny talent for blowing absolutely freaking everywhere, so be sure that you're wearing work cloths and more importantly, that you're nowhere near your house, car, or anyone else's belongings when you're tackling this project. It is 100 percent not worth it to spray paint these amazing chairs yourself if you then have to pay someone else to repaint your car. You will not forgive yourself, I promise.

Another note: Regardless of how much you want to get this project done on a rainy day—DO NOT GIVE IN TO TEMPTATION AND SPRAY PAINT INSIDE YOUR HOME. Everything I've just mentioned about spray paint going everywhere is exponentially more true if you're inside—not to mention that your home will smell to high-hell for days afterward. Don't do it. Put a drop cloth out in your yard, on the roof of your apartment building, in the street for god sake—but DO NOT SPRAY PAINT IN YOUR HOUSE. It will be a sticky, miserable, stinky mess you'll regret immensely.

Okay, now you can really start: Give your spray can a good solid shake with the cap on—for at least 30 seconds—before you start painting. Then, remove the cap, and holding the spray can nozzle about 6" away from your furniture, begin spraying in consistent, smooth motions from left to right. Try to evenly coat the piece, but don't go buck wild here. Your results will be far better if you go back and do a second coat than they will if you end up with dripping, gunky looking spray paint that takes forever and a day to dry; so if you need to do a thin, even layer; and then circle back—that's the way to go.

Now that you've done that . . . Once you've thoroughly coated your furniture with a layer of paint, allow it to dry completely. Check the spray can for the recommended dry time to ensure that it's fully dried before start fooling around with it again. After your first coat has dried, flip your furniture over and spray any of the areas on the underside that you missed on the first round. In my experience, I find that the best way to catch these hard-to-see-spots is by putting your piece on top of a table or work bench (covered in a drop cloth, unless you want that to be lime green too), but obviously that depends largely on the size of the furniture you're painting and the amount of space you've got to work in.

The boring part: Repeat. Yep. Depending on how thoroughly you were able to cover the original finish in your first round of spraying,

you may need to repeat all of those steps again. Some brands of spray paint recommend a light sanding in between coats of paint, and they'll also tell you how long they think you should wait in between coats—so make sure you consult your spray can to make sure that you're getting the best possible results out of your street find.

While we wait . . . While your frame is drying, you can turn your attention to reupholstering your seat cushions. This project is seriously a cinch, but aesthetically, it separates the boys from the men. By simply adding a customized cushion to your junky street chair, you've truly transformed it to a whole new piece of furniture. And honestly, it's so easy to do, you really don't have a good excuse not to.

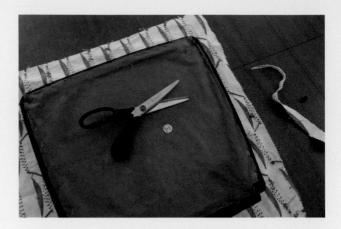

Start by laying your fabric out, pattern side down, on a clean, flat surface. Lay your seat cushions (which you removed during the "prep work phase") on top of your fabric, with the cushion side facing down and the wooden side/ underside of the seat facing up.

Now for those pinking sheers! Using that wonderful pair of pinking sheers you bought because I told you to (or just a really sharp pair of scissors because you're not ready to commit to a life of home improvement), cut out your fabric, leaving a roughly 3" border around the size of your seat cushion. When in doubt, leave a bigger border than a smaller border, as you can always trim the excess later. The 3" I've estimated above is determined by the depth of your seat cushion, so if it's a relatively slim seat cushion, 3" should be ample, but if it's astoundingly plush (a.k.a. tall) you might need to leave more. Before you cut, test how much extra you'll need by pulling your fabric around the cushion base. Don't skimp. It'll screw you in the end if you haven't cut the fabric large enough.

TAKE NOTE: Before you cut your fabric, make sure you pay attention to how the pattern runs and how the cushions attach to your chairs. For example: if you have a striped fabric like

the one we're using in this project, make sure you line the pattern up correctly on all of your seat cushions, so that when you put the cushions back on the frames, the holes will line up with the original holes in the base, and the pattern will still go in the direction you want it to on ALL of the chairs. This can take a little finessing, but take the time to do it before you staple the fabric in place, so you don't have to drill new holes in the base later . . .

Almost finished . . . Once you've cut out your cushion fabric, it's time to use your staple gun to fix the fabric in position. Pull the extra fabric border of fabric tightly over the edge of the cushion and onto the wooden base of the cushion. Holding the fabric firmly with one hand, and then use your other hand to staple the fabric into place, stapling every 2" to make sure you get a nice tight fit across the seat cushion. If your seat is round like ours, you may need to overlap the fabric slightly so that it hugs the seat base tightly. Channel your paper-airplane skills from years past and you can figure out how to fold the fabric without too much difficulty. If you can't, maybe you should reconsider your life as a DIYer and head to your closest Target instead.

The End! Now that your seat cushions are recovered and your chair frames have dried completely, you can reassemble your glorious chairs! Put your seat cushions, face down, on a smooth, clean surface (ideally a table or work bench that isn't covered in spray-paint residue) and then position your chair frames directly on top of your upside-down cushions, with the seat back coming down below the table top. (That's kind of a difficult image to describe: Imagine you were going to mop under your table—how would you put the chairs on top of the table so that you can mop? Ooooo-kay. Now you get me.) Make sure that the screw holes from the frames are directly in line with the screw holes in the seat cushions, and then re-screw each of your screws tightly through the chair frame into the cushion base. (Aren't you glad you didn't lose any of your screws!?), and now flip your chairs back over. Ta-da!

How Large Should Your Rug Be: a.k.a. "How Large Is Your Budget?"

The size of your rug, ideally, would be dictated by a couple of fairly obvious things. The first: the size of the room. The second: the placement of the furniture in that room (obviously the placement of your furniture is going to be directly influenced by the room it's in, so it's kind of chicken-or-the-egg in terms of which comes first).

However, for many of us, the size of our rug is more frequently dictated by our budget than by our preference—so you've got two things to figure out: 1.) How big should your rug be? 2.) Can you find something affordable in that size? And I hate to be a buzz kill, but 100 percent of the time, I'd rather see an understated, unremarkable rug (a.k.a. IKEA SISAL!) that fits the room and the furniture properly than see, like, an utterly gorgeous antique Persian rug (worth SO MUCH money) that looks like a sad doily sitting on your living room floor because it's vastly too small for the room. I'm sorry. I don't care if it's valuable. I don't care if it's beautiful. Put it somewhere else. Put it in a hallway. Use it in your bathroom. Turn it into a wall-hanging for all I care. Seriously, a rug that's too small for the room just looks like a sad, small rug—an island in a sea of flooring and furniture—no matter how beautiful. So, if you're working with a super tight budget, the solution is to buy an inexpensive, uneventful area rug that's actually the appropriate size for your room. Earlier in the book I discussed finding a balance of "pop" and "quiet" planes in your home . . . Letting your rug be one of the "subdued" moments in your room provides a subtle backdrop for other jazzy accents, while also saving you a couple of bucks. That's a win-win, I'd say.

Now then: How to Determine an Appropriately sized rug:

Whether or not you're encumbered by a miniscule budget, you still need to determine the appropriate size of your rug for your furniture arrangement. I like to start by looking at the size of the largest piece of furniture in the room, as that will have a huge influence on your rug size. For example: In your living room, you want the rug to be proportionate to your sofa. In your bedroom, you'll want it to be in scale with the size of your bed. Those are simple sentences, but actually figuring out what's "to scale" is a little trickier. Let's delve deeper . . .

For Your Living Room

Remarkably there aren't that many ways to arrange your living room furniture unless you're living in some sprawling suburban palace/nightmare. Obviously there's loads of variation in there, big chairs/small chairs, love seat/ sectional but more or less, you're either anchoring your sofa against a wall, or you're floating the whole arrangement in the middle of the room.

If you're anchoring the sofa against a wall: This is, from the perspective of buying a rug, a less expensive arrangement, because you need less rug to make this work well. Ideally, you'd buy enough rug so that the front two legs of all of the furniture lands comfortably on the rug. In this scenario, I'd recommend deciding where you'd

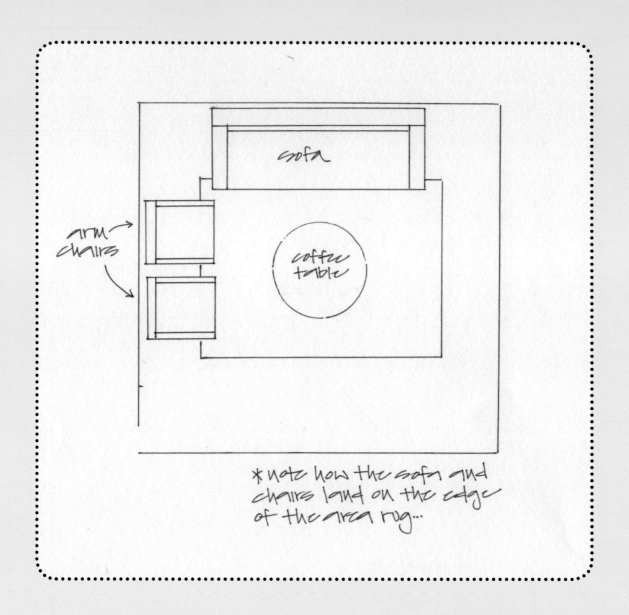

arm → chairs

sofa

coffee table

*note how the sofa and chairs land on the edge of the area rug...

like to place your furniture, and then measuring for your rug, rather than doing it in reverse, as you run the risk of ending up with furniture much farther apart or much closer together based on rug size rather than comfort.

The reason this is less expensive is basically you're buying a rug only slightly larger than the width of your sofa, plus whatever chair arrangement you're working with.

If you're floating the furniture in the middle of the room:

My preference for this configuration would be that you use your rug to create a "room within a room," basically your rug is an island that contains all of your furniture, so all four sofa legs will land on the rug; all of the chair legs will land on the rug; everything that makes up your primary living room seating area sits on the rug. So you can see

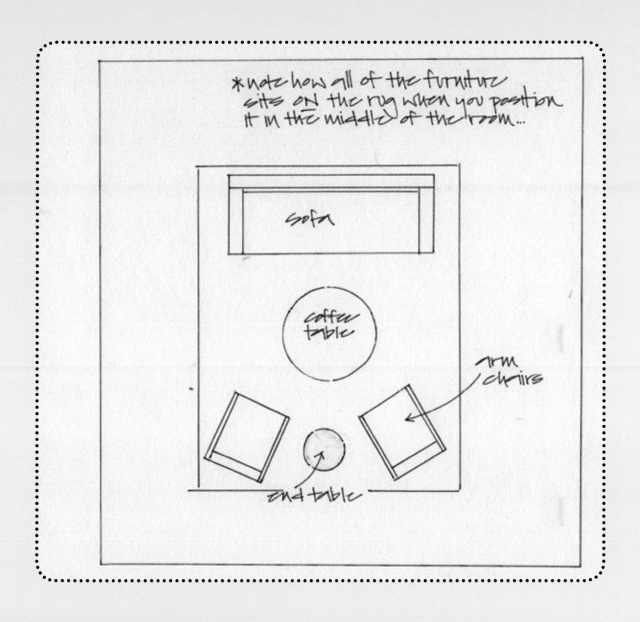

how this arrangement would end up being more expensive—you'll need a rug that's larger to fit completely under your sofa and chairs, rather than just perching under the feet of your furniture.

To be clear, I am not suggesting you configure your room based on the rug you can afford. I'm suggesting you configure your room based on how your furniture fits best, and then find a rug you can afford that will fit appropriately.

For Your Bedroom

Your bedroom rug should be a little more straightforward. This is based on the size of the room, but hypothetically, my first preference would be that your bedroom rug lands about 9" away from the wall at the foot of your bed, and a similar distance from the walls on the left and right sides of your bed. If you've got a wide dresser, the rug would ideally land under the front two feet of the dresser, or (push comes to shove), 6"–9" in front of the dresser's feet, and you're still in great shape. If you've got a tall narrow dresser, we're back to Plan A—with the rug landing about 9" away from the wall.

A big no-no, which I see surprisingly frequently, is putting the rug all the way under your nightstands. Not only is this unnecessary, but it's also kind of weird looking. When you're determining the size of your rug, measure a few inches in front of the front feet of your nightstands, so, depending on the depth of your nightstands,

about 21" inches away from the wall behind your headboard.

If your budget prevents you from getting an area rug that lands 9" away from the walls, there's a Plan B. An alternative method which will also work: Measure your rug so that it protrudes at least 36" on either side of your bed and at least the same amount at the foot of the bed. The idea here is that you don't want the size of the bed to overwhelm the size of the rug, so that the rug looks like a dinky little footnote at the bottom of your huge bed. So even if you can't afford to buy a rug that will fill your room,

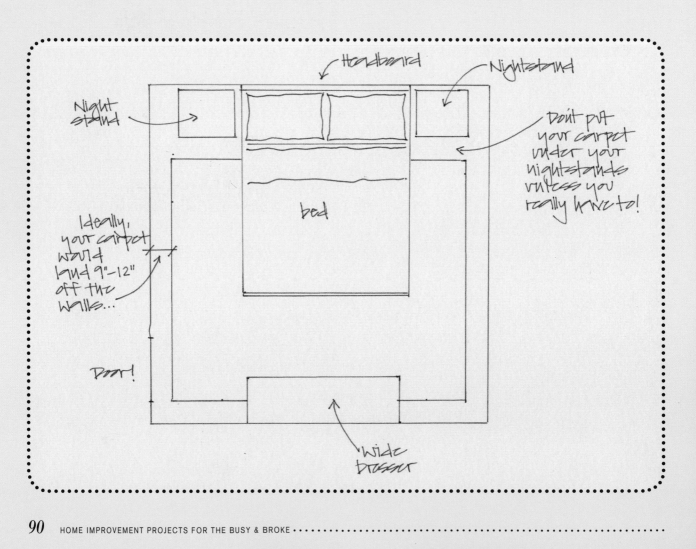

you can still buy a rug that will look reasonable with your bed.

And I know it's annoying that so much of the rug is under the bed. I know it's annoying that you are paying for rug you aren't seeing and to that I say, "Tough luck." This is how it's done, buddy, and this is what will look good, so stop being a whiner and go buy a rug that's the appropriate size for your bed.

Wait! There's a Plan C: Emergency-Super-Duper-Broke-Rug-Plan: Runners!

If you really can't swing the cost of a proper area rug for your bedroom, consider buying a pair of runners to go on the left and right sides of your bed. DO NOT BUY ONE FOR THE END. They should be close to the length of your bed, still land a couple of inches in front of the legs of your nightstands, and for the love of Pete, invest in non-skid rug mats, or you and they will be slipping all over the place!

How to Build and Upholster an Ottoman

Ottoman vs. coffee table

It's an ongoing dispute: an age-old debate of comfort versus practicality. Obviously it's nicer to put your feet up on an ottoman than to put them on a table. And it's definitely better to put your coffee cup on a coffee table than an ottoman. Especially when you inevitably spill coffee everywhere. So you'll have to decide—are you on the comfort team or the function team? I can't make that decision for you, but I can teach you how to transform a crappy old coffee table into a totally awesome ottoman. Which is great if you want an awesome ottoman.

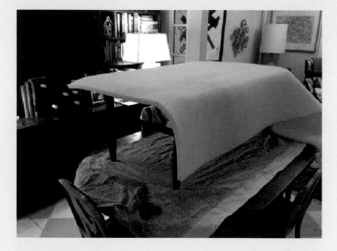

Skills you'll need: Virtually none. Just basic proficiency with a staple gun and the patience to wrap the foam and fabric around the table. We're talking E-A-S-Y, people.

Time you'll need: Maybe 30 minutes, tops.

Stuff you'll need:

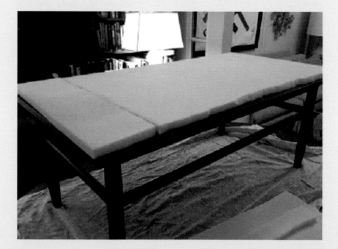

- A coffee table of your choosing. I think something leggy and wooden seems to work particularly well, but I bet a cool steel base would be great looking too. This is a perfect project for a Craigslist/yard sale/street find, though if you find a coffee table with really terrific legs—and what you want is an ottoman, this is a perfect project for that piece too.
- Rad fabric: I needed only 1 yard of fabric to cover my 45" x 24" coffee table.
- Foam/batting: I used two layers of thin memory foam, and a layer of thin felt batting, but if you hit

up your local fabric/craft store, you could probably get away with just buying 2" foam and you'd be in business. I've even seen 2" foam available at Home Depot, so that's another resource to check.

• Staple gun and staples

Get yourself set up: I'm a firm believer in being able to see my projects when I work on them, so I started this bad boy by putting the coffee table up on my dining room table, so I could really see what I was doing. Don't forget to protect your dining table from the feet of the coffee table, or you'll end up making another, considerably more difficult project for yourself.

Then I stretched my foam over the coffee table, and figured out how big of a piece to cut. Based on the piece of foam I had, I was able to do two layers—one the size of the table top, and a second layer on top, that I cut to be about 3" larger on each side than the size of the table top. The amount of foam you choose to use is up to you—I wanted my ottoman to be plush and comfy, so I went with two layers, but theoretically, you could skimp on this a little without terrible results.

Up to bat: Yep. I just made that pun. Don't judge. Once my foam was in position, I lay the felt batting on top of the layers of foam. The batting is an extra step you can skip if you're really doing this on the cheap. It helps keep the fabric in position, and softens the squeakiness of the foam underneath, but if your options are dinner or batting, definitely buy dinner.

I cut my felt batting so that it draped over my foam by a couple of inches, so when it was time to staple it, the felt batting was the outside layer—holding everything under it in.

HANDY HINT: When I started stapling, I put a couple of staples in with my staple gun, in order to keep everything in place, and then I flipped the whole kit-and-kaboodle over, and stapled it upside down. This made the stapling way easier, allowing me to get a better, stronger angle for stapling without having to reposition everything once it was flipped over.

Keep going . . . Once you've got the table flipped over, use your staple gun to secure the various layers of batting and foam in place onto the underside of the table. I stapled the hell out of the foam and batting to make sure it didn't shift around. Dealer's choice on how thoroughly you fix this in place. If you're sure your table is a complete piece of junk, you could also apply glue to the table top to keep the foam in position. I'm a big believer in versatility, so I decided not to glue it, in case I wanted it to convert it back into a coffee table sometime down the pike.

Pretty much the last step: Now place your piece of fabric on top of the ottoman, making sure to position it so that the pattern is straight, and then trim down the excess so there is only 3" overlapping each side, just the way I did with the foam and the felt batting. Then repeat the method above—popping in a couple of staples and then flipping it over—so it can sit upside down on your work surface/dining room table.

No, really! You're almost finished: Now insert your row of staples, just the same way you did when you were fixing the foam in place. At the corners, you may need to fold the fabric slightly to get the tightest corner. Don't go too fast-and-furious into that section—take a second to figure out which fold gets you the flattest, least visible results—and then staple it in place. Once you've stapled everything, flip that baby over, and you've got yourself an eye-catching, wicked-comfortable ottoman that will function as one of your homemade POW! moments in your living room! And if you're like me, and still want a place to put your coffee, pick up a cute tray at your local home-goods shop, and your ottoman will be able to function as both coffee table and comfortable foot rest, all in one!

How to Make Your Own Upholstered Headboard

You can do this. And you should!

The upholstered headboard is the unsung hero of every bedroom. It is the much-needed punctuation that gives definition to both the bed and the wall behind it, by creating a visible, structured distinction between the two planes, adding texture and nuance, while also giving a purposeful, "designed" quality to your bedroom. Also it's really comfortable to lean against. Basically, what's not to like?

So now that we've agreed that the upholstered headboard has a lot going for it, the question is: How are you going to get one? To be honest, there are a ton of super cheap versions available online—you can troll around online and probably find something of decent quality for $150–$300. Make no mistake, this won't be a glorious piece of high-quality furniture, and definitely not produced in the United States—but if the country of origin doesn't bother you, the quality doesn't need to be phenomenal to do the job, so if you're not feeling crafty, shell out for a ready-made one and call it a day.

Personally, I'd rather spend $150 on dinner than $150 on a headboard, so I'm going to make my own headboard, and use the money I saved for a night out. Maybe my priorities are skewed, but let's ignore that for the time being . . .

The "How-To" of upholstered headboard making is pretty simple and pretty cheap, especially if you've got some spare fabric laying around. You'll need about two yards of fabric, and in the interest of keeping this project as simple as possible, you want to choose a fabric that can "run" in either direction. Basically that means you need to choose either:

a. A solid fabric without a pattern.

b. A pattern that won't look weird if you run it from left right instead of up down because otherwise you'll have to sew two pieces of fabric together and this starts becoming more work than it's worth and that cheap-o beige headboard from Vietnam starts looking a little more appealing.

Skills you'll need: Very few!

Time you'll need: A medium amount of time, maybe an hour or two, depending on how handy you are and how helpful your local lumber supply is.

Supplies you'll need:

- 2 yards of fabric
- 2 yards of 1" thick foam
- 2 yards of cotton batting
- 1/4" plywood for headboard, size determined by the size of your bed.
- Full-size: 57" width x 30" height
- Queen-size: 62" width x 30" height
- 4 pieces of 1" x 6" wood cut to size to make a frame within the piece of plywood, so if you're making a full-size headboard, you'll need:
- Two 1" x 6"s, cut to 57" long
- Two 1" x 6"s, cut to 18" long
- 3 Heavy-duty picture-hanging D-rings (I doubt you know what this is, but if you go to a hardware store, they can show you.) Look for the ones with 2 or 3 screw holes, to make sure it can be securely connected to your headboard.
- Electric drill w/ Phillips-head drill bit
- Heavy-duty staple gun & staples
- Wood screws for connecting the 1" x 6" to the plywood, and the D-rings to the 1" x 6"s. Once again, if you're not sure, ask at the hardware store for recommendations on size and strength . . .

All righty. It's an intimidating supply list, but making this baby is gonna be a breeze. Let's get in there!

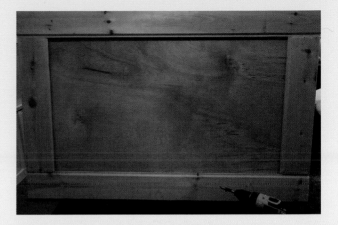

I'm like a broken record here, but I always think this is the most important step: figure out where you're going to put this sucker together. Clear a space on your floor or put a drop cloth over your dining room table, and then you can really get started. Start by laying out your frame, configuring the two 57" pieces horizontally, and separating them with two 18" pieces, positioned vertically. Basically you're arranging a flat box on your floor. Pretty straightforward.

Ideally, you'll then be able to lay your plywood panel on top of this box and it will line up tidily to the edge of your plywood panel. If this is the case, you can go ahead and screw through your plywood panel into the 1" x 6" frame you've laid out, using roughly six–eight screws per side to make sure that bugger is really attached to your frame. If not, straighten up your "frame" so all of the sides are parallel and flush with the sides of the plywood, and then attach.

Once you've got your plywood attached to your 1" x 6" frame, you're like 75 percent finished with this project, so we're moving right along . . .

Next up: Cut your 2 yards of 1" foam so it's the same size as your plywood panel (57" x 30" for a full) and then lay out the 2 yards of batting on your flat surface. Then place your 1" foam on top of the batting, and position your plywood panel and frame, face down, (a.k.a. frame-side up) on top of the foam. The foam should now be

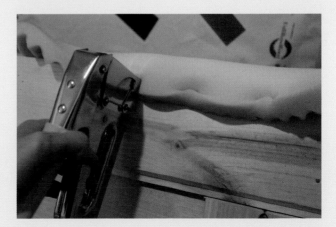

parallel and flush with the edges of the plywood, just as the frame was before. Now pull the batting around the edges, and using your staple gun, affix the batting to the frame. Be thorough here—use plenty of staples to make sure the foam stays in place, and trim the excess batting as needed.

So now you've got a really soft rectangle of wood.

Lay your fabric on your flat surface (iron it if needed before you attach it permanently to a piece of wood!) with the front side of the fabric facing down. **Make sure if there's any pattern you're working with that you've got the fabric positioned so the pattern will be straight once you're finished. **

Pull the fabric taut around the edge of the foam and batting, and then staple that excessively to the wood frame on the backside of your headboard. Okay, maybe not excessively, but you want it to be really tight so it doesn't wrinkle and tug over time, and you also want it to be really well-attached or the fabric will pull and fray in the places where there are staples, which would be a real bummer.

Once you're finished, you'll attach your D-rings! You want to attach your D-rings next to the fabric and batting that's been pulled around the frame, so that it doesn't end up sticking out further than the fabric. So—to be clear—not on the fabric, but next to the fabric, closer to the center of your wood panel. Position the three D-rings equidistant from each other on the back of your headboard, and make sure all three D-rings are also positioned at the same height on your headboard, so you don't drive yourself nuts hanging it up.

And finally . . . installing your headboard! This is probably the hardest part of this whole headboard-building endeavor, because the installation will be specific to the kind of walls you have. If you have hollow walls, you'll probably want to use heavy-duty "hammer anchors" to secure three screws into your wall, to hang your D-Ring hardware on. In my case, I have old brick walls, so we are using three lead anchors to secure the screws in place. The most essential step to this is making sure that you're using the right hardware for your particular walls (ask at your local hardware store if you're not sure!) and then—making sure that your screws are positioned correctly so that your headboard will hang in the right place, and look/ be level.

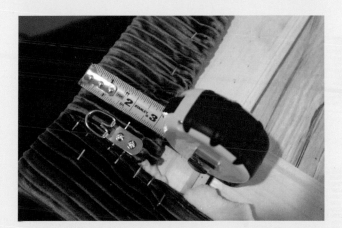

The key to this is an oldie, but a goodie: Measure twice, drill once. Except in this scenario, where I'd recommend measuring six times, and drilling thrice.

How to Dress Your Bed so You Feel Like You Live in a Hotel

So we've talked about this a little already. I seriously believe in a beautiful, comfortable bed. I am a major subscriber to duvet inserts, feather-blend pillows, high thread counts, fluffy euro shams, tailored bed skirts, and linen duvet covers. And you might be a big fan too, if only you had any idea what I was talking about. Let's start with some vocabulary words, so you can familiarize yourself with the some "bedding terminology" to ensure that we're on the same page moving forward:

Duvet insert: This is a fluffy blanket that goes inside a duvet cover. These are typically washed twice a year—when you get it out in the Fall and when you put it away in the Spring (or you can use it all year round, depending on the weight and warmth of your duvet insert).

Feather-blend pillows: This refers to the kind of filling that goes inside the pillows. My preference is absolutely for feather or down pillows, as they make me feel like I'm sleeping on an opiate-filled cloud, but obviously this is a personal decision. Be aware that if you have certain allergies, feather pillows and down duvet inserts might make you itch like crazy, so be sure you know what you're getting into before you fork over the money for these bad boys. Feather pillows also look great—they have a perky fluffy-ness that looks polished and tidy on a well-made bed, which is another perk.

Poly-fill pillows: These are the typical alternative to feather pillows, and let me assure you—they are not all created equal. A good quality poly-fill (or "down alternative") pillow can feel so much like a down pillow, you'd barely notice the difference—a bad quality version feels so much like sleeping on a stack of bricks that by night number three, you'll be burning it in the street. Don't cheap out here!

Thread count: Okay, thread count is an important term in the world of bed sheets. Thread count refers to literally the number of horizontal and vertical threads per square inch of your sheet. Generally speaking, the higher the thread count, the softer the sheets—or more to the point—the lower the thread count, the more your sheets feel like sandpaper. There is something to be said for aiming in the middle of this range—like a 400–500-thread count, as higher thread count usually implies that the sheets will wear better over time, and even soften with use. That said, I've also bought some terrific 300-thread count sheets that I've been totally happy with. Don't get me wrong, you wouldn't mistake them for 800-threads in a million years, but the difference between 300- and 400-thread count sheets can be negligible, in comparison to their difference in cost, which can be noticeable. My advice to you is to make the decision based on touch. Actually open the sheets and feel them. I've done this before and found 500-thread count sheets that felt like (revolting) slippery nylon, and I've found 200-thread count sheets that felt like opulent 600-thread count-ers; so you never know until you give 'em a feel.

Euro sham pillows, more pillows, and other pillows.

I love pillows. All of them. I want as many pillows on my bed as humanly possible. It's truly laughable. Verging on ridiculous. But when I'm laying there for the seven-and-a-half free minutes I have to read each evening, and I'm leaning against my headboard, resting against a puffy euro sham, ensconced in pillows in every direction—I am utterly blissed out and entirely unfazed by your mockery.

So—for your reference:

Euro sham: 26" x 26" pillow, usually put behind the standard pillows, leaning up against the headboard.

Standard pillow: Ordinary 20" x 26" pillow, which gets a regular pillow case. This goes in front of the euro sham and behind the standard sham.

Standard sham: Ordinary 20" x 26" pillow, which gets a more decorative pillow case. (People often don't sleep on their sham pillows.)

Lumbar pillow: If you're fancy, you can also have lumbar pillows on your bed. These are typically 16" x 26" or 14" x 22", but sometimes can be double width so that it runs the width of your bed. These are really optional—but I like the pop of color my lumbar pillows add to my bedroom set up.

Throw pillows: Last one, I swear. The throw pillow is your little "pizzazz pillow." It's the one I add to my bed to provide a little contrast and play in relationship to my bed linens, so that everything feels a little more collected and curated, and a little less "matching set of everything." That said, I'm clearly giving my bed linens more consideration than most people—so you can skip this if it feels like it's overkill.

Bed skirts: A bed skirt is the piece of fabric that drapes over your box spring, between your box spring and your mattress to hide your box spring and whatever you're keeping under your bed. There are many different styles of bed skirt, as far as I'm concerned—unless you're decorating an older home with an antiquated aesthetic, you should pretty much only use a tailored bed skirt. In my book, anything else is just unnecessarily frilly and overly-decorative. And generally, I like them to be as neutral as possible, so it doesn't compete with or limit your bed linen choices going forward.

Duvet covers: The last piece to complete your bed is your duvet cover or comforter. Personally, I think comforters are totally gross—they remind me of half-clean motel rooms near highways in the Midwest, and I diligently avoid using them. If you insist on using one, fine, but there's no way you're getting my stamp of approval. A duvet cover, on the other hand, makes me think of breezy, light-flooded resorts overlooking the Caribbean. A duvet cover is essentially a removable envelope of fabric that your duvet insert fits into, which keeps your duvet insert clean, and allows for easy washing of your duvet cover. I don't know what the science is behind this—but I swear duvet covers just feel lighter and more fresh—literally more "breezy" than a comforter. Investing in a couple of duvet covers is the way to go—worth every penny to create that "hotel retreat" experience in your very own bedroom.

Coverlet/quilt/throw: This is really the last thing I'm going to suggest you put on your bed, I promise. I happen to really love a coverlet—it's essentially a very thin quilt or blanket that sits toward the end of your bed, to break up the color or pattern of your bed linens, to add a little extra warmth on a cold night, to curl up under when you want to read a book in bed, but you don't want to entirely make your bed again, and for me, it's also a great buffer layer between my (smelly) old dog

and my lovely (clean) bed linen. It is absolutely optional—so if you're at the end of your patience or your budget, you can give this one the skip and I won't think less of you.

So I know that sounds like a lot of pillows, a lot of blankets, and a lot of money, but I want to be crystal clear about one thing: I exclusively buy my bed linens from discount home shops like TJMaxx and HomeGoods, or from places like West Elm and Macy's when they're having an extra-sale-on-a-sale-and-free-shipping-sale. I have a thirteen-year-old dog, a three-year-old child, and a very busy husband; which translates to a lot of things that ruin sheets and very few things that care about sheets. I'm not going

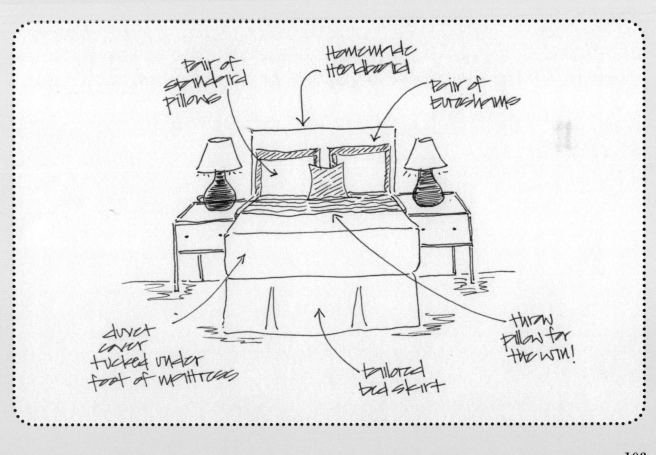

to fork over $200 for a freaking duvet cover. That's just bananas. My dog is going to make it hairy, my kid is going to wipe sticky hand prints on it, and I'm going to be way too busy to fastidiously dry clean everything in order to make it crisply immaculate again. I just can't stand the pressure. But when my pretty gross old dog lounges around on my $20.99 sheet set; I just strip it off and throw it into the wash along with all the other stuff my family has sullied. Not a care in the world.

My point is, your bed can look and feel like a hotel bed without costing you a small fortune. And in my opinion, unless you're really loaded and don't plan on owning a dog, it definitely shouldn't cost a fortune, because there are more important things to spend your money on.

Okay, so now that you know what is going on your bed, you need to know how to set it up. We're going to work from the ground up, and then you can refer to the diagram if this just isn't clear enough.

STEP 1: Position your bed skirt. Your bed skirt should be evenly placed on top of your box spring, below your mattress, so that the three sides that drape down hang evenly above the floor. One side won't have a draping piece—that goes toward your headboard so you don't see it.

STEP 2: Now to make your bed. Start by pulling on your fitted sheet. If you're using a comforter, you might also use a flat sheet. I can't stand that sheet, but if you insist, put that on next, and tuck about 12" of the sheet under the bottom end of your mattress to keep it in position.

STEP 3: Now get your duvet cover and duvet set up. I recommend grabbing the upper two corners of the duvet cover from the inside and pulling them out to meet your duvet. If you've recently bought a duvet cover, you'll most likely find little ribbons attached to those upper two corners. Those are there so you can tie your duvet insert to the top corners of your duvet cover, and it will keep your duvet in place while you're using it. This is a very basic but astoundingly useful development in duvet-cover technology. No kidding. It's revolutionizing the way beds look. Once you've got your duvet insert positioned, shake the duvet cover down over it and button up the closure at the bottom. If you need to give it another shake to get everything evenly distributed, do it now, because it's way harder once you've tucked it under your mattress.

STEP 4: All right—now you're going to tuck your duvet/duvet cover under the mattress the same way you did your sheet (if you insist on using a flat sheet). So you'll pull the duvet down about 12" past the foot of the mattress and then tuck it tightly under the mattress. Pull it snugly up over the mattress so it lays crisply flat.

STEP 5: Pillow time. (I'm going to assume you've decided to commit to as many pillows as I've got, but obviously only follow instructions for the pieces that apply to you). You start by positioning your euro shams up against your headboard. All of the pillows should sit fairly upright, at like an 80 degree angle from the bed. Once your euro shams are in place, position your standard pillows, also at an 80 degree angle. This is an important detail—for some reason people put their pillows parallel to the earth and your whole bed just fizzles out. Don't do it. Go for that crisp, perky look by setting them up right. One hundred percent better. Now, place your lumbar pillows in front of your standard pillows, and if you're really going for the gold, casually toss on your throw pillow. I'm not kidding. I don't want it to look like it's saluting me—which, come to think of it—is kind of what I want the rest of the pillows to look like. I want that throw pillow to be more laid-back, a little more nonchalant. I know it's annoying when I give throw pillows human characteristics, but humor me and give it a try.

STEP 5: Coverlet? If you decided to go with the coverlet, first let me say, "Good call." So—where to put the coverlet? What you should do is fold your coverlet into thirds, and then place it toward the foot of your bed, so it leaves about 9" of duvet cover showing at the end of the bed, and then comes up about 24", leaving the rest of your bed uncovered toward the headboard. As I mentioned earlier, the coverlet is a lovely way to add another layer to your bed—it breaks up the color or pattern of your bed linens and adds a little extra texture to your set up.

Very opulent hotel!

Fast-Track Bedroom

If there's no way you're gonna do that other stuff . . .

1. Buy new sheets and duvet, and wash. Wash is a crucial step here because nothing says, "I only bought these sheets to impress you" quite like the folds leftover on a set of sheets when you've just taken it out of its packaging. This matters less if your parents are coming over, but if you're trying to wow a potential love interest, those folds sing "desperate" pretty loud and clear. I mean, it's kind of cute too, but then again, I'm a sucker for the underdog—not all romantic prospects will be so easily charmed.

Okay, sheets bought, washed, bed made.

2. While you're at the home store buying sheets, consider buying a pair of bedside lamps. Or if that feels too cookie-cutter for you, take a foray onto Craigslist to see what you can find. However, don't forget expediency is crucial in this scenario. I know you'd wanted to find bedside lamps that were the perfect physical manifestation of your remarkable, charismatic, wildly individualistic personality, but you screwed the pooch, bud, because now you've got four days to get your apartment sorted out and those perfectly-emblematic-just-right-for-you-lamps aren't likely to show up just in the nick of time. Let's leave it at "buy bedside lamps" and you can decide what you've got time for—just as long as you're able to check that box off before your visitors arrive.

3. Wait. Maybe #3 should proceed #2—and I'm giving you too much credit. I'm assuming you already have bedside tables at this point. If you don't have bedside tables, tackle that first, and then address the absence of lamps. Do not put your lamps on the floor unless, miraculously, it's 1980, you live in a loft in Soho, and your mattress is also on the floor.

At this point, things should already be improving in your bedroom pretty distinctly. You've got new sheets, bedside tables, bedside lamps . . . Now what's happening with your windows? Tell me you don't have a bed sheet taped in your window. Or worse—literally closed in your window so that a little piece of it is actually dangling OUTSIDE. Tell me that isn't what's happening. Hopefully you've got an uncharacteristically beautiful pair of blinds providing you marvelous light filtration throughout the day and night. But let's go ahead and guess that's probably not happening. If we've got really limited time until your family gets here, at least take the decaying sheet down. I don't care if it's bright in your bedroom, or if you've got a crap view of a brick wall, or better yet—a good view directly into someone else's apartment. In my book, there is only ONE excuse for hanging a sheet in your window. A baby. Yep. Only when you have a baby are you allowed to be so desperate for room-darkening effects that you can hang a sheet in the window. If you don't have a baby, tough it out and let's find a permanent solution instead.

Before you decide on one of the following options: DON'T FORGET TO MEASURE YOUR WINDOWS. Not just inside, but also the height from the ground. Refer to the next section for the specific things you need to measure. *Do this properly the first time to save yourself the anguish and annoyance of multiple return trips to perfect your window treatments.*

Option 1: Go to IKEA. They have an epic and very affordable collection of window treatments and drapes which you can hang up NOW. Don't forget to buy the rod hardware while you're there, and when in doubt, always buy too long rather than too short. We'll talk about why in he next section, but in the meantime, just do it. I know they're more expensive. Tough luck.

Option 2: Go to a home improvement store like Lowes or Home Depot. There you can also buy drapes and rod hardware. Their selection can be a little less reliable/modern than IKEA's but I've had successes there too, so don't rule it out. Or— if you really want to cheap out—you can get them to custom cut roller shades for you, right there on the spot. Getting customer service at Home Depot can be like pulling teeth out of your own face with tweezers, but it can be done, and at twenty dollars a pop, can be worth the energy to make it happen.

Option 3: Wait for it, because this one is a surprise: JC Penney. "What?," You say, "JC Penney is still a thing?" Yep. Surprise! JC Penney is still in business, AND they do great custom window treatments. Roller shades, solar shades . . . The drapery is a little less reliable, but if you've got the time to wait for delivery, JC Penney's custom roller shades are the deal of the century! You can usually find a coupon code or sale to combine with their already staggeringly low prices, and lickity split—you've got completely customized roller shades coming at you through the mail, for about twelve dollars a window. Best. Price. Ever. Make no mistake, they're no Hunter Douglas or The Shade Store in terms of quality, but they're about one-tenth the price, so that seems like a more-than-fair compromise as far as the cost to quality ratio is concerned.

Option 4: All right, fancy pants. You've actually got $120 to spend on window treatments. And to be honest, it's worth every penny if you've got the pennies to spare. Buying custom shades from somewhere like The Shade Store is completely awesome. The quality is great, the options infinite, the turn around is usually about ten days to two weeks. Free shipping. What's not to love? I know I sound like an advertisement, but really—The Shade Store is just as good of a deal as JC Penney if we're looking at their cost to quality ratio. What that means is that although they're more expensive than JC Penney, they're also much better quality and come with many more bells and whistles than the JC Penney shades. They also come with much better customer service than the JC Penney shades, so although you're investing more in the short term, you're getting something that will last you longer in the long term. So, I guess this depends how "long term" you're feeling. If you're definitely headed for a new neighborhood next time your lease expires, JC Penney will do the trick. If you're sitting pretty as a home-owner or a long term renter, it might be worth it to take the plunge. You decide.

Icing on the Cake:
Time to Accessorize

How to Hang Your Drapes Like a Pro (Even If You're Tight on Funds)

If you go online right now and Google "How To Hang Your Drapes," you'll come up with all sorts of tips to make your window treatments look their best. And to be fair, it's solid, though maybe slightly elitist advice:

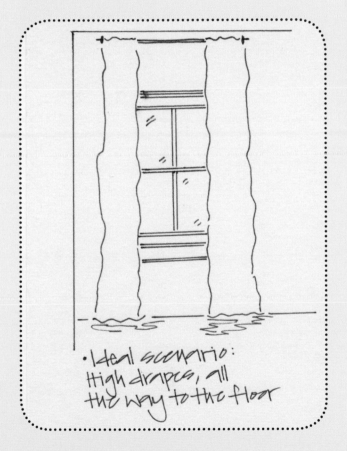

•Ideal scenario: High drapes, all the way to the floor

- Hang your drapes as high as possible to emphasize the height of your room. (True.)
- Be sure you're buying drapery that is full enough for your windows—ideally two times the width of your windows. (Also true.)

- Focus on your hardware. Beautiful hardware is a part of the complete package. Don't overlook buying better hardware to complement your beautiful draperies. (Yeah. Okay.)

Those are all delightful tidbits if you've got an ample budget for your window treatments, and if that's the case, follow that advice to the letter. But if you're like me, you're shopping for drapes at IKEA for a reason—not because you just love their Scandinavian inspired bird print collection, but because they're inexpensive.

So if you're in the same boat as me, and you're trying to stretch your budget as far as humanly possible, you're going to have to follow a different set of rules.

FYI. Drapes, curtains, and panels are the same thing. One just sounds fancier than the others.

If it's really not in the cards monetarily for you to buy drapes that will run from floor to ceiling, there are a few "make-the-best of it" solutions that you should consider, depending on just how tight your budget is.

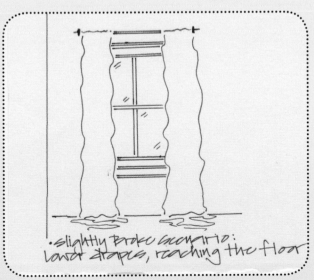

•slightly broke scenario: lower drapes, reaching the floor

A. Slightly broke: So you're strapped enough that you don't want to fork over $49.99 a panel (and those are IKEA prices!) but you're willing to take a bit of a hit in the name of beauty. Rather than having your drapes float a foot off the floor, which really does look like you're anticipating flood waters, you can consider buying the tallest panels you can afford that will run from the floor to anywhere above the window. I know it's "recommended" that they reached all the way up to your ceilings, but c'est la vie—you've also got to pay rent, pay off your school loans, and eat, so if it's that or "recommended drapery," I'm happy hanging your drapes 3" above the top of your windows (tell yourself you'll have nicer curtains when you finish paying off your school debt). This will not make anyone scream out in horror when they come to your home, and any reasonable interior designer will confirm that it's better to be 10" from the ceiling than 10" from the floor.

B. Pretty freaking broke: Resist the temptation to hang curtains from the top of your windows to anywhere shorter than the window sill. I really wish you didn't have to hang your drapes just IN the window, but if it has come to that—it's preferable to starvation, bankruptcy, or awkwardly short curtains. But if you can't swing hanging your drapes from the top of your window down to your sill, turn to a third option.

C. Completely broke: All right, so you're really trying to make this work, but to say you don't have much expendable income is an understatement. Consider the charm of "cafe curtains." The cafe curtain is hung ideally half way up your window on a skinny little (inexpensive!) curtain rod, and it hangs from halfway up the window down to your window sill.

D. Penniless: One last option, if you're desperate for some privacy on your windows and you just can't part with the cash for drapes: consider roller shades or even adhesive paper that covers your windows. You can pick up roller shades at your local hardware store, and can often have them cut down to fit your windows

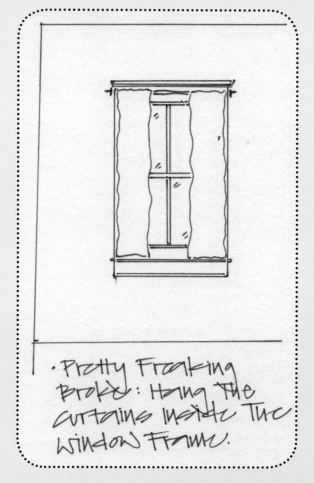

· Pretty Freaking Broke: Hang the Curtains inside the Window Frame.

• completely broke: go for the "cafe curtain" for a little privacy and a little money.

Now, on to the other two pieces of "advice"—As far as I'm concerned, snippet #2 (about the width and fullness of your curtains) is absolutely true and resounding difficult to control when you're buying ready-made drapes. Whoever decided on the standard lengths of drapes was also in charge of estimating the standard width of the windows they hang on, so you're kind of stuck with what you get. I wouldn't let this drive you too bonkers unless you've got crazy wide windows which will look laughably silly with stringy little drapes hanging on each end. If that's the case, and you really need drapery with greater fullness, you could consider buying three or four panels and asking your local tailor or laundromat to sew them together. If your budget is tight, cut panel 3 in half vertically, and sew the cut edge to another full (uncut) panel. This will add another 50 percent width to each side of the window, which isn't necessarily optimal, but it's definitely better than nothing.

And regarding that last word of wisdom: About your hardware . . . Your drapery hardware will be visible. It's true. And you definitely don't want it to be so flimsy that it bends or breaks. However, it also doesn't need to be an emblem of your design prowess, or more to the point, it shouldn't be. With a sincere apology to the ornate metal workers of the world, your drapery hardware does not need to have kook-a-doo curlicues at the ends of it. It doesn't need seed glass orbs suspended in a nest of wrought iron. No flowers. No fleur-de-lis. None of that gobbledygook is worth the up charge of having it. Put that extra money toward having longer drapes and keep your hardware as understated as possible. Let your drapes do the talking.

exactly at the store. If that's still too costly, consider buying frosted adhesive paper that affixes directly to the glass of your windows. I'm not saying it's gorgeous, and you're not likely to see it featured in a design magazine, but it's still significantly better than taping, stapling, or worse—wedging—a flat sheet up in your window. Come on guys. You're better than that.

Making Really Great Drapes, on the Cheap

Ambitious, but you can do it!

There are certain things that just cost so much in home improvement. I'm not sure why exactly—but every once in a while there's just an outlier—something that seems to be so much more expensive than it needs to be. And window treatments are just such an anomaly. Truly, assuming you've got any windows of reasonable size (worse things can happen, I assure you), it can cost a small fortune to get window treatments, particularly if they're custom-made. This project is an affordable solution to that conundrum: making your store-bought "least expensive-drapes-available" appear custom-made; without the horrifying price tag. When you consider that the real deal runs over one hundred dollars per drape, and yours cost about forty dollars for a set of two, you'll be more than motivated to make them yourself!

Skills you'll need: A decent amount. Not huge, but you'll need to be at least moderately competent with a sewing machine, or have really nice parents/friends who are . . .

Time you'll need: This will be a gradually dwindling number. Initially, you'll probably need about 30 minutes for one drape, but once you get the hang of what you're doing, this will get progressively easier a.k.a. faster.

Additional advice:

1. Don't get discouraged by drape #1

2. Don't try to make a whole apartment of these in one sitting unless you're really comfortable with a sewing machine and aren't prone to furious tantrums when you encounter adversity with a sewing machine (I am not that person).

3. Don't only make drape #1, or your windows will look worse than they would have if you'd just hung up your cheap IKEA curtains.

4. Perseverance folks! It's usually what separates the triumphant from the quitters (well, that and skill).

Tools you'll need:

- Plain canvas drapes (check your local big box store or IKEA to find these on the cheap. Right now I'm loving IKEA's Ritva drapes. They're not only perfect for this project, but they're pretty darn nice solo too—made of a medium weight, slightly coarse cotton-y canvas which provides a decent amount of light filtering without looking too heavy and dense.)
- Numerous rolls of 1"–2" grosgrain (solid colored, cotton) ribbon, in the color of your choosing. In this project, I used a 2" grosgrain to add a bold

punch to the drapes, but I've used a 1" thickness before with very pretty, more subtle results; so dealer's choice there.

- Sewing pins.
- Measuring tape or ruler.
- Thread to match your grosgrain ribbon.
- Access to a sewing machine!
- Pinking sheers or sharp scissors.

(I'm like a broken record about these pinking sheers, but really—they're great! They discourage the ribbon from fraying, so your stitching will last much longer, and so will your drapes.)

IMPORTANT: Before you head to your local fabric/craft store to buy the ribbon, figure out how much you'll need. You need at least the length of each curtain times two, for each panel, plus a little extra, so if your curtains are 84" long, you'll need ≈175" for one panel, or 350" for a set. You may also want to plan ahead and buy your ribbon online. You'll find a far larger selection of colors available online, and will also have an easier time finding large quantities if you're doing multiple windows.

*PLANNING AHEAD: I know you're gung-ho to get started, but first you must pre-wash your drapes before you sew the ribbon onto them, even if they're brand new and completely clean. Follow the cleaning instructions exactly, to ensure that your drapes don't shrink up in the wash.

Okay. Now we can start: I highly recommend starting by finding yourself a nice, big work space. If you don't have a sprawling dining room table, consider moving your furniture aside and doing this project on the floor in order to give yourself sufficient space to really spread the drapery panels out flat. Begin by measuring out the ribbon for the first drapery panel. Measure the length of your panel, and then add an additional 3"–4" inches, so you can fold the ribbon over the top and bottom hem of your drapery panel. So for instance, if your panels are 84", you'll cut an 87" length of ribbon.

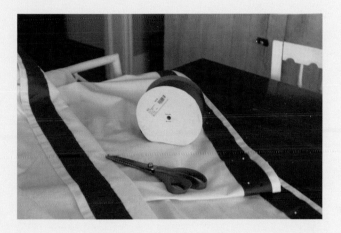

Getting going: Position your ribbon where you'd like it on the drape. I placed my ribbon about 1" in from each vertical hem, on both the left and right sides of each panel, but if you're looking for a place to pinch pennies, you could just do one line of ribbon, on the inside-side of both panels. While it's not as effective as two ribbons, it will still give your drapes a "pop" at half the price, so don't rule it out if your budget is tight or your time is limited. Once you've decided on your positioning, start pinning your ribbon in place, measuring frequently to make sure that you've actually got a straight line. When you insert your pins, they should run parallel with the ribbon (up-down on the curtain panel) so that when you start sewing, you can sew along-side the pins rather than driving over them. Make two rows of pins on each ribbon, one fixing the right side of the ribbon into position, one fixing the left.

Oh God. The hard part: I have a contentious relationship with sewing machines. I started my sewing life using a really jacked up older machine that used to break down, devour my bobbin thread, and snap my sewing needles perpetually, so I've got a little PTSD at this point. However, if you're using an even moderately functional sewing machine, this shouldn't be a soul-wrenching experience, so I'm crossing my fingers for you. Once the ribbon is pinned in place, you can jump into sewing. Thread your sewing machine with the matching thread you bought to match your ribbon—making both the bobbin and the lead thread the same color.

And then just start: Using your sewing machine, sew two vertical lines, running parallel up the very edge of each side of the ribbon, going from the very bottom to the very top. When you start, fold your ribbon over the bottom hem of each panel and sew it in place as you go, and when you get to the top, fold your excess ribbon over the top hem and sew that into place too. Once you've sewn both sides of the ribbon completely, you can remove the jillions of pins and you're finished with drapery panel #1! Not too bad, right?

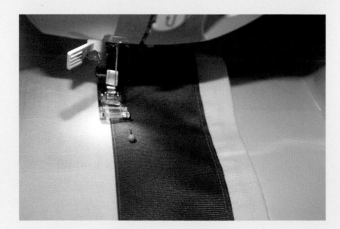

**And then repeat these steps a million times
. . .** So the one bummer is that you'll have to
repeat this project two to four times, per window,
depending on how many ribbons you afix to each
drape, but the silver lining is that it's really
more time consuming than it is skill-intensive,
and once you're finished—ba-da-bing! You've
got truly fantastic looking drapes for a fraction
of the typical cost. One last step to seal the deal:
flip your panels over and iron the ribbon and
panel from the back side. This will give your
drapes a nice, crisp look without damaging or
stretching out the ribbon. Nice work, folks!

The final step: Unfortunately, final step is
essentially "repeat all previous steps" for each
additional drapery panel you need. This can be
a playful, but inexpensive way to unify multiple
rooms in your home (for example, doing custom
panels with matching ribbon in your living room
and dining room . . .)

Just Dim It

Seriously people. This should be one of the first things you do when you move into a new home. If I was considering a new tattoo, "Just Dim It" would be in the running—it's that serious. As far as I'm concerned, surgical theatres and dentist's offices are pretty much the only places that wouldn't benefit from a dimmer. Kitchen: Awesome to have a dimmer. Bathroom: Awesome to have a dimmer. Bedroom: Really awesome to have a dimmer.

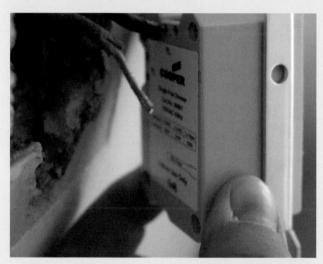

There is no reason you shouldn't be able to easily create instant mood lighting everywhere in your home. Think about what it's like when you go to a restaurant. Not McDonald's—I mean a real restaurant. With nice napkins. What's the bathroom like in there? Dim, soft, ambient. You know why? Because that feels nice. You don't want to go from a delicious dinner with friends, basking in the relaxed ambiance of a "dimly lit" dining room and then get assaulted by the full intensity of a 100-watt bulb when you need to pee. It's just not nice.

However, when morning rolls around and you're back in that same bathroom and you need to pluck your eyebrows, you're going to be so happy you've got that blaring 100-watt bulb to help you see. And that, my friends, is why you need a dimmer switch in the bathroom. This will cost you roughly fifteen dollars and will be an imperceptible pleasure whenever you've got guests, or basically anytime after 5:00 p.m. Just dim it.

Now roll up your sleeves and let's get cracking!

First things first, and this is a serious step. **Let's not electrocute ourselves**. I can't emphasize that enough. It's no fun and can potentially kill you, so start by turning off the power to your light fixture by going to the electrical panel and switching off the power to that room. Double check that you've disconnected the power by using a voltage tester to make sure there is no electricity traveling to the switch.

Unscrew the original switch from the wall, double check that the power is off with the voltage tester and then use a screwdriver to disconnect the two wires connecting the wall to the switch.

Now here's the tricky bit: Once you've removed the two wires from the old switch, you're going to connect them to the new dimmer by inserting each wire into the dimmer box. After you've securely inserted each wire, wrap the entire affair in electrical tape. If I were going to make a list of the most important rules of home improvement, "There's no such thing as too much electrical tape" would make the top ten. When in doubt, electrical tape.

Your dimmer will obviously come with directions, so follow those to the letter, but the gist is as it is depicted above: "Disconnect the old switch, connect the new switch. Wrap in electrical tape to make sure you don't burn down your house. Re-install into wall. Turn power back on."

How to Change a Light Fixture without Electrocuting Yourself (an Important Distinction)

You'll need:
- Wire stripper/cutter
- Drill and/or screwdriver
- Wire nuts
- Electrical tape
- (Voltage tester to be super safe)

Skills needed:

Low-medium skill (Comfort with a drill would be ideal, but not required)

Time needed:

About an hour, probably less, but give yourself a buffer in case it's tricky to get the new light fixture up.

The most important part of "Not Electrocuting Yourself"—turn off the power. Locate your electrical circuit panel and then determine which circuit breaker controls the room where you'll be working. Switch that circuit off and confirm that the light is no longer functioning. If the circuits in your panel aren't labeled, turn on the existing light you're planning to replace, and then turn off the power to each circuit until the light in question goes off. Leave the power off, and label this circuit breaker for future reference. (Do this. It will take you two seconds and next time you're changing a light fixture, you'll know it isn't that switch.) Just to be thorough, turn off the light's wall switch as well.

If you don't have access to your electrical panel or you're feeling less than sure about whether the power is off, invest about fifteen dollars in a voltage tester. I'd like to emphasize again the importance of not electrocuting yourself in pursuit of a nice apartment. It just doesn't seem worth it.

Time to remove the old fixture: Remove the cover of the old fixture by unscrewing the screws or nuts holding it fixed to the ceiling. Once you've removed the cover, you'll be able to see the wires attaching it to the ceiling.

HELPFUL HINT: Snap a photo of how the old fixture is connected to the wires coming from the ceiling with your phone so you can refer to it when you're connecting the new fixture.

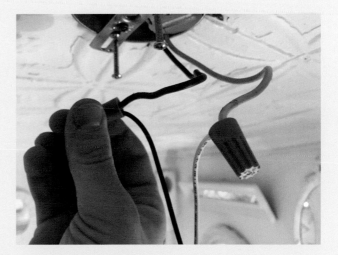

Remove the old wire connectors, and then untwist the fixture wires from the installed wires in the ceiling. It's probably something simple like the black wire is connected to the black wire and the white to the white. But if you live in an apartment remotely as glamorous as our Brooklyn tenement, your apartment has seen its fair share of shady contractors, so you might find something less than typical up there . . .

Also, you may have to remove the cross bar that's holding your old fixture up. I know I'm a broken record, but make sure you keep all of the old screws someplace easy to find, like a cup, so they don't roll away while you're installing the new fixture. Because you just never know if you're gonna need 'em. Like I mentioned, your new fixture may not be compatible with whatever dubious ancient electrical box they stuck up there twenty years ago, so having the old screws might be the difference between success and failure.

Now, check the stability of the existing electrical box in the ceiling. You may just need to tighten a screw or two to make it secure again, and it's definitely worth doing before you put up your new fixture, only to discover it's hanging cock-eyed. And obviously there's no point in installing that lovely antique fixture you just found on Craigslist, only to have it fall to the ground and shatter.

Then you connect the new fixture. If you're installing a new in-the-box fixture, it probably came with instructions. Read those to make sure you install your new light fixture correctly. But the gist for most fixture is this:

- Install the cross bar, and then attach the white wire from your fixture to the white wire in the ceiling, then the black to the black (some older fixture wires aren't color coordinated, so just attach one fixture wire to the white in the ceiling and one to the black).
- You may need to use the wire stripper to cut your wires to size, because you don't want too

much excess wire up there or the ceiling cap won't fit over it. Once you've cut your wires to the correct length, use the wire cutters to remove a little bit of the rubber insulation and expose about a thumbnail's worth of bare wire. Hold the two wires you want to connect side-by-side, slip the wire nut over them, and then twist until tight. Then cut yourself about a finger's-length of electrical tape to secure the connection (start by wrapping around the wire and wind your way up to the tip of the nut, so that the wire nut is firmly held onto the wire).

This is the shitty part: secure the new base or canopy. At this point, your new light fixture will be sort of dangling from its wires, attached to the wire in the ceiling, so you need to have your drill or screwdriver handy, ideally in your pocket or on top of your ladder. Gently fold the connected wires up into the electrical box or into a void in the base or canopy and use the included hardware to attach the fixture base or canopy onto the crossbar in the electrical box. This can be a really fussy, frustrating process, getting your new fixture lined up with your old electrical box. You can do it, but you're going to have to be patient, and if you can get someone else to support the fixture while you finesse attaching the cap, it will make your life considerably easier.

Once you've got it securely attached, you can screw in a light bulb, flip the breaker back on at

the electrical panel, turn the light switch back on in the room, and you're finished! Congratulations. You've just installed an electrical fixture and lived to tell the tale.

*Just to be clear: It really isn't that perilous to install a light fixture. Odds of killing yourself doing it have got to be pretty low, or I'd be toast by now.

What's in a Pillow?

So the first question: why do you need throw pillows at all? Think of them as the lipstick of your living room. Yeah, your face is okay without it, but throw on a little lipstick and your face looks 100 percent better. (Okay, this analogy may not apply to everyone reading this, but you get my drift. Work with me here. Have you ever tried to come up with analogies that apply to EVERYONE?) The point being—pillows function not only to make your living room more comfortable and inviting, but also a punctuation mark—an opportunity to add contrast, layers, and depth to the design of each room. Designers LOVE pillows. I'd put pillows in the bathroom if I could find a reasonable way to do it. They are another way to add dashes of pattern or color into a room, to extend that "curated feeling" without overwhelming the room with an abundance of that color or pattern. Basically, they're the best.

Let's be perfectly clear. The actual filling and SIZE of your pillows make a difference. Tiny pillows look like sad forgotten blips in the ocean of your sofa. They look uncomfortable and unwelcoming. Pillows that are too big? They look like bedroom euro shams, misplaced in your living room, overwhelming your sofa and preventing any potential occupant from leaning back or getting comfortable. Size is everything.

Next: Filling. As far as I'm concerned, you should only ever use down & feather filled pillows. I'm a real fascist about this. Honestly, I barely care if you're allergic to down. Power through it! Don't be a whiner. What's a little rash/blocked breathing passage in the name of interior design?

If scale isn't a concept you think you've mastered at this point—when in doubt: nothing smaller than 18" unless it's a really dainty settee (that's the same as a loveseat); nothing larger than 20" unless, I don't even know what, unless it's a massive deconstructed ten foot sectional sofa (Google "Ligne Roset" to see an example of this.)

But I guess if it's really going to drive you straight to an inhaler, you could consider a high quality polyfill insert. You can tell the difference between good and bad polyfill because when you squish a good polyfill pillow, it still feels vaguely downy. It compresses, it's comfortable, and it doesn't feel like someone has shoved a polyester track suit inside a pillowcase. Although you will definitely find that down or good quality polyfill pillows are a little more expensive than the cruddy stuff, try to be discriminating. I mean, not if it means you can't eat dinner tonight, but if you can squeeze out the cash for a couple nicer pillows from your local discount home store (probably twelve dollars a pillow?) you'll thank me in the long haul.

So, the last question is, buy 'em or make 'em? If you're in the early stages of home improvement, you can probably stand to buy your pillows at a local home store. There are so many other DIY projects to tackle—make your life easy and just buy something readymade. You'll need to be picky—pillows at discount shops are frequently made of garish, tacky fabrics with yucky polyester (track suit) filling. But a little patience and hunting usually reveals a couple of fun/pretty options that will suit your aesthetic.

If you're feeling like you're really nailing this home improvement thing, and you're ready to explore the world of sewing, making your own pillows is an awesome place to start. It's a fairly simple project so you can learn how to get comfortable with a sewing machine without tearing your hair out, and it opens up a huge world of fabric options you wouldn't necessarily find at a HomeGoods.

The other perk of making your own pillows, if you've got the emotional stability to get it done, is it allows you to coordinate your various fabrics to get a personalized, custom aesthetic you're not going to see at anyone else's house. If you whip up a couple of pillows and then reupholster an ottoman in a fun complementary fabric, you've really upped your game significantly.

Stuff you'll need to make your own pillows:

- **Fabric** (Usually one 54" width yard is enough to make one 20" pillow; and one-and-half yards should be enough to make two 20" pillows.) This number will vary somewhat depending on how neurotic/precise you want to be about lining up and centering your patterns. I wish I was more dedicated to this, but I'm usually more concerned with my budget.

- **Pillow inserts** You can get pillow inserts online, from regular home stores (Bed, Bath, and Beyond!) or you can buy ugly pillows from the TJMaxx clearance shelf, toss the hideous covers, and pull the pillow inserts out for your gorgeous custom pillowcases. This will allow you to buy the nicest possible inserts for the cheapest possible price. I bet you can guess where I buy mine.

There are two minor downsides to making your own pillows:

1. It will cost a little more than buying readymade. Are you thinking, "What? But I'm making it!" Nope. Custom fabric costs more than pillows that were mass-produced in Taiwan. Sad, but true.

2. Depending on your sewing machine, making pillows might be a little bit aggravating. I'm probably not supposed to confess this, but about 70 percent of the time, my sewing projects start with me, five minutes in, either raging or crying. I'm the proud owner of a truly-demonic, eternally-busted sewing machine from hell, and I swear that almost every time I get the bloody thing out I have to rebuild it from the inside out. Most of the time I eventually prevail, but not before I've sworn off ever sewing again. Hopefully, if you're at the stage where you're interested in sewing your own pillows, you've found a sewing machine that actually fucking works, and you're already in better shape than me. The reason I'm telling you about these temper tantrums is not to impress you, obviously, but to prepare you. Sewing has a learning curve (evidently one I'm still ascending) and it can be incredibly frustrating. But, it can also be marvelously liberating, because once you've gotten comfortable sewing, there are a limitless number of projects you can complete yourself. And that's when you'll start saving yourself some money.

- **Access to a sewing machine** (ideally with the correct color of thread.)
- **Sewing pins**
- **Needle and thread** (also with matching thread, ideally.)
- **Pinking shears** (I know. I always tell you to use pinking shears. It's true that scissors also cut, but let me reiterate that what's great about pinking shears is that they help prevent fabric from fraying, which is particularly good with something that gets a fair amount of use, like sofa pillows. And because it really sucks when you finally finish sewing something and then it falls apart because you didn't use fucking pinking shears. I promise.)

Okay, I think we've talked this thing to death. Let's get cracking.

First, you've got to measure out your fabric. I recommend taking the measurement of your pillow insert (let's say it's a 20" square insert) and adding an additional 3" to the total width and length. Cut two 23" squares out of your fabric. If you're feeling nut-so, you can try to line up the pattern so that it's the same on both sides or if you like, you can try to center your pattern. As I mentioned earlier, I don't really care about this stuff—it tends to waste more fabric than it's worth in my opinion. I haven't really figured out how/why I would look at both sides of the pillow at the same time, so I'm not totally sure why anyone cares about lining up the pattern, but I'm sure a fancier designer would insist this was important for some reason. We've already established I'm a little laissez-faire, so if you want to be anal, be anal. No judgement here.

Once you've cut your two 23" squares, it's time to pin the pillow. You're going to pin the pillow to create a border to follow with your sewing machine, so it's important that the lines you pin are fairly straight, and the correct measurement, or you'll end up with some weird trapezoidal pillow and you'll be really bummed out.

What you're aiming to do is make your actual pillow about 1" smaller than your insert (this will make it look full and fluffy) so once you've cut your fabric into two 23" squares, you're going to pin the two pieces together (with the front side of the fabric facing in on both sides), to make a 19" square with your pins. This should leave you about 2" on either edge. When you're putting the pins in, you should put them in perpendicular to the edge of the fabric, so when you sew with your machine, you're running the machine parallel to the head of the pins, not over them. I forget this every time when I'm pinning, and then have to yank them out as I go. Do not follow this example.

Perpendicular! Perpendicular! Perpendicular!

Now for the really hard part: Sewing.

Or, now for the easy-breezy part because you own a modern sewing machine which actually does what you tell it to. (I hate you.)

If you're familiar with sewing, you probably know what you're doing and you can take it from here. If this is your first dance with sewing, I recommend that you start about 4" in from the left bottom edge. Position the fabric in your sewing machine so that you head toward the left edge, following the pins. Depending on your school of thought, you should start by running the sewing machine back and forth a couple of times right at the beginning, so your stitching doesn't unravel, but that might be a trick my mom taught me that isn't how the pros do it (but it works).

Now carry on sewing toward the left edge, and when you get past your perpendicular line of pins, hang a tight right turn (clockwise?) and start following your pins (parallel to the edge) toward the next corner above. If you've done what I've just described, you should have sewed a capital L-shape basically. Once you get to the

next corner of your pins, make another right turn, and head across the top of the line of pins. If all is going according to plan, you should be making a capital C-shape at this point. When you get to the next corner of pins, take another tight right and head down the right side of the pillow. At the bottom, take a final right turn and head toward the short stitches you made when you started. Again, go about 4" in from the edge of the fabric and stop. Do the back-and-forth stitching again so this last leg won't unravel.

If you've followed my instructions correctly (or more specifically, if I've written my instructions correctly) you should have stitched an open O-shape, with about 15" of un-stitched fabric between the two short sides on the bottom.

Now remove your fabric from the sewing machine. Using your pinking shears, trim back the excess fabric on the outside of your sewing line. Don't cut it too too short or you run the risk of it fraying (yes, even though you used pinking shears!) but trim it back so there's about ½" of fabric on the outside of the entire (open) square you sewed.

Now turn your pillow case right-side out, so the pattern is showing on the outside. Stick your fingers into the pocket you've made and push the corners out, so you get nice sharp corners on all four sides. If you need to take an iron to your pillowcase because it's looking a little rumpled, now's the moment, because once it's got a pillow insert in it, it'll be a heck of a lot harder to iron.

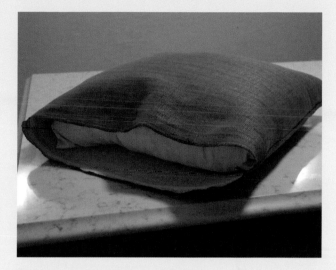

Now for the most challenging part: You've got to ram your pillow insert into the 15" opening you left un-sewn. I recommend rolling the pillow up, kind of like it's a newspaper or a burrito, and then feeding it, skinny ways, into the opening, but do whatever you've got to do to get it in there without ripping your opening larger. Try to go gently as you do this because it's best if you don't rip your stitching open.

Once you've got the insert in there, stick your hand inside the pillowcase to make sure that the corners of the insert are tucked up into the corners of your pillowcase. And now it's time to seal her up.

Take the two remaining flaps of the pillow case and fold them inside the pillowcase so they're in line with the seam you stitched. If you need to, use a couple of sewing pins to keep the flaps inside the pillow while you're sewing. Now, using your needle and thread, you're going to sew this little flap closed. You can use a couple of different stitching methods—you can use tiny little stitches that are hard to see but a little bit tedious, or something called a "Ladder Stitch" which is another great way to make your seam invisible. If you decide to go down that road, I'd recommend googling it for specific instructions, because me writing them out for you is going to make both of us crazy.

And that's it! You just made your very own pillow. To hell with HomeGoods! You got this.

What to Hang, How to Hang It, and Where to Hang Your Artwork (Such That It Is) in General

One is the loneliest number that you'll ever do . . . Unless you've got big art.

There are a couple of important aspects to hanging artwork:

- where?
- how big?
- how high?
- how many?

And often, the answer to all of those questions is found by looking at the size of the piece. Mastering the concept of scale can be the clearest, easiest way to determine where, how high, and how many. Tiny art over big furniture looks lonely, basically like you ran out of money by the time you got around to buying artwork. But big furniture with nothing above it looks pretty lonely too, so ideally, you'd find a solution in the middle—either grouping a collection of smaller art, or shelling out for something a little less dinky—maybe aim for a 24" x 36" or even larger if you can afford it (and fit it.)

Obvious places you should be hanging artwork:
- above your sofa
- above your bed
- over your sideboard or dining room credenza
- above your dresser

If you've got a limited amount of art, focus your resources on the places that are the most glaringly empty. Rather than spread your collection of tiny art work throughout your apartment, which basically makes each piece feel like a tiny island in a sea of wall, cluster your small pieces together—the sum of the pieces will read like one larger piece and will occupy the wall more comfortably than dribbling them around your apartment, like tragic little splashes. This just highlights your shortage of art work. (Flip ahead to page 133 for more hints.)

Places you shouldn't hang artwork:
- above your TV
- generally around your TV unless you've got a strong plan for a gallery wall which will incorporate your TV, or if the wall is large enough that you can hang something substantial near it.

How High?

I like to hang my art work a little high, probably because I'm a little taller than the average lass. I tend to place the center of the frame about 12" below my eye level, so for me, that's about 4'6" for the center. Obviously this is dictated largely by the size of the frame, but if we're talking medium sized (say 24" x 36"), I would hang it so the top will be 5'6" off the ground. This is also influenced by what's below it, so don't quote me as saying there is one "right height" for art—it's dictated by so many other factors—the size, what's below it and around it, what room it's in.

It's not as simple as "always hang something this high"—that's rubbish. That's like saying "Only ever buy an 84" sofa." Without knowing your art and your space, I can only give recommendations. I "recommend" that you don't hang a singular piece of tiny art above your sofa. I "recommend" you don't spread your artwork like miniscule forgotten islands all over your home if you don't have much of a collection. If you haven't yet collected much artwork, try concentrating your art collection in one space—ideally the most public space in your home. I'd rather see your living room feel complete and let your bedroom feel a little sparse for the time being, because A) Your bedroom should be a more serene, restful, zen (a.k.a. empty) place anyway. And B) Your visitors shouldn't be nosing around your bedroom anyway. Unless you want them in your bedroom. In which case, they shouldn't be looking at the art!

What to hang?

Okay, this is a tricky one, because I've already spent pages campaigning against hanging just any ol' crap up on your walls. And obviously you know how I feel about tacking shit up with push pins (DO NOT DO IT). But at the same time, I don't want you to psych yourself out when I use the word "artwork." I'm not talking about valuable, or museum quality, I'm talking "stuff you like, in frames you put on walls." Odds are good if you're reading this book, you're a solid five-ten years from owning truly valuable art work, but for the love of Pete, please don't wait until then to hang anything up. The kind of artwork we're talking about here can be found anywhere—scour flea markets and yard sales, troll Craigslist and Etsy, visit holiday art markets and burgeoning coffee shop galleries. Ask friends to make you pieces, frame things that aren't traditionally art—street signs or your grandfather's army cap. Put 'em in a deeper frame, and hang it up! You should be looking for/shopping for pieces that resonate with you—pieces that fill you with something when you look at them, because you're the one who is going to be looking at them most. If there's one thing I would discourage you from buying—it would be museum posters. I know. I'm sorry, it's disappointing. They're cheap, they're big. But take it from someone who has professionally hung up SO MANY peoples' art work—they just don't hold up. They yellow, they date. And suddenly you've just got this crappy old poster—and I don't mean "crappy old = vintage," I just mean poor quality/obsolete. And it's not like anyone looks at those posters when they're hanging in someone's apartment and thinks, "Wow. That's so exotic. He saw Van Gogh at the Met last year." Along with thousands upon thousands of other people . . . Come on. You can do better than that.

How to Hang a Gallery Wall

Take advantage of IKEA frames to make it the best that it can be.

If you already know you want to hang a gallery wall, you can skip over all the chit-chat, and go straight to the part where I talk about how to frame it, how to hang it, and what to frame. However—you might not even know why you'd want to hang a gallery wall. Basically the idea behind the gallery wall is it allows you to display a wide variety of "art" (a loose term) in a way that feels purposeful and curated.

This is not going to be a politically correct segment, so if you're easily ruffled, and/or firmly believe men and women are created equal on all things, you should probably skip forward to the next section. You're not going to like what you're about to read here. Your sensibilities will be offended. And yep, we're still just talking about hanging a gallery wall. Nothing more ideologically charged than that. With no further introduction, let's jump in:

When I met my now-husband, he was just a young buck. His bed was unmade, his surfaces were littered with 40 oz. bottles, and his walls were covered with a wide array of posters, articles he'd cut out, and witty things he'd accrued: a Mets snow hat, a piece of a taxi sign, a toll bag from the subway in the nineties . . . Clearly he was a catch.

If, at that moment, I had suggested he head to the nearest IKEA to frame all of his assorted "art work," in order to create a unified, aesthetically pleasing (while still intellectually stimulating) gallery wall, I probably would have been shown the door. And to be honest, I left him to his own devices when it came to designing his personal space for many years. But when we decided to move in together, I put my foot down. Gently, but firmly. Because while I was unwilling to live in a world surrounded by beer bottles, I also wasn't trying to crush his autonomy or force him to live in a world of pale pinks and sea foam greens. I just wanted to take his style and find a way to meld it with my style. So I headed to the local craft store and bought a dozen black frames, all different sizes, some slightly different than others, and I framed all of his witty tchotchkes and "hilarious" articles. His taxi sign got a frame, his toll bag got a frame, the photo of him with "his boys" got a frame . . . And then I hung them all up kind of helter-skelter along one wall, and ba-da-bing! Future-husband–friendly gallery wall. His contents + my style = harmony at home.

I'm sorry if I'm underestimating the male population, and worse—I apologize to my husband if I'm underestimating him—but I just don't think most men under forty give a shit about how their stuff is framed, or if it's framed at all. Hopefully they feel a little more invested in their surroundings if they've been reading this book. Maybe they really will realize the transformative power of putting everything in a frame, but odds are good, ladies, this responsibility is going to fall to you. And not just for your romantic interests—you'll probably need to step in for your brothers and single friends too. I'm sorry if you don't like it, but the cold hard truth is the vast majority of men just don't care about this kind of home decorating minutia, but it can make the difference between designed and dorm room, so it shouldn't be overlooked. You'll just have to take charge. Or give good instructions.*

There are a couple of ways to do a gallery wall. Okay, there a couple hundred ways to do a gallery wall, but if you're looking for a sure thing, it's better to limit it to a few:

Option 1: Unifying modern frames with a wide variety of contents. This can be the perfect solution for a case of "Boy Wall."

Option 2: Assorted, related eclectic frames with a common element (many different styles and textures, all make in gold guild, or all green, or all black carved wood, or whatever). If your frames are varied, I recommend unifying the contents with a theme: maps, fruit, horses, vintage advertisements.

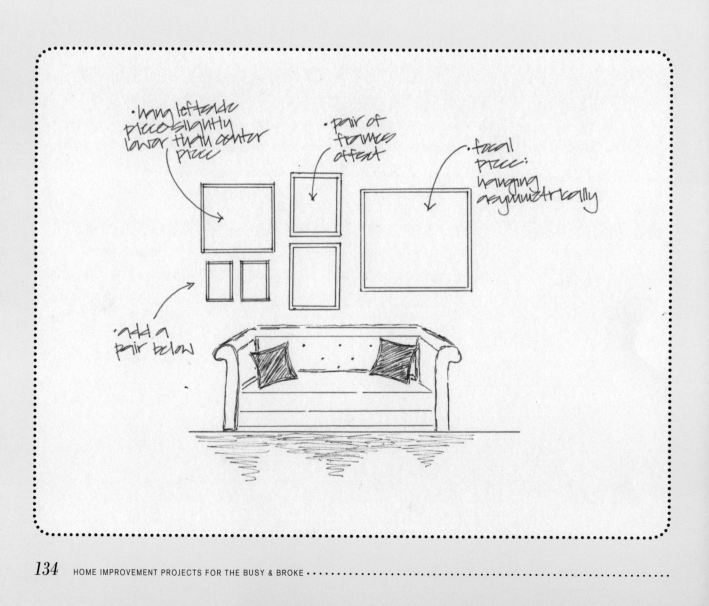

Option 3: Combination of option one or two, with the addition of unframed textural/sculptural pieces—like decorative plates, jewelry, collected fabric, etc.

To be clear, option three is definitely the most challenging version of the gallery wall, because it requires a careful balance of frames and tchotchkes, hung "just so," so that it has a curated air about it, rather than a "random shit hung together on a wall" air about it.

And now to discuss contents:

With Option 1, you have an opportunity to really play around. By framing everything with the same or similar frames, it allows you to explore a variety of mediums and textures without sacrificing a purposeful "designed" aesthetic. Consider incorporating photographs, sketches, paintings of all varieties (oils, watercolors, abstract and realism, you name it). You can even frame objects—bracelets or badges or whatever else you find meaningful or interesting—and the very presence of the unifying frame will elevate your situation drastically. Basically it's taking the same crap your boyfriend pinned on the wall using tape and push pins, and reorganizing it so that it creates a curated wall, rather than looking

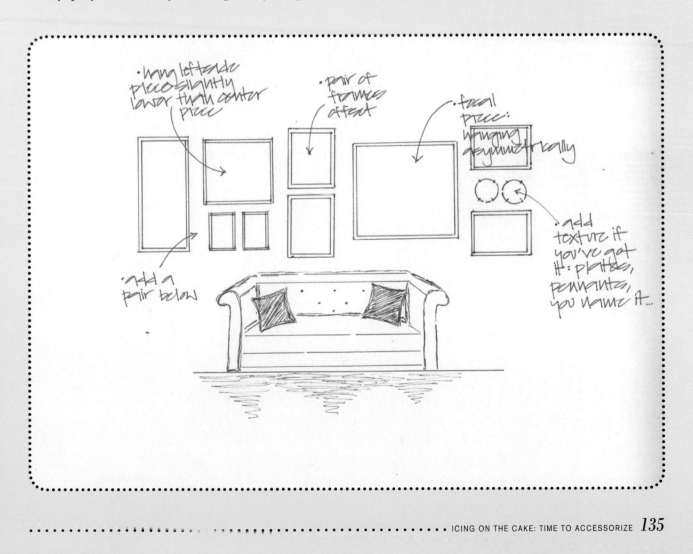

like a wall where trash has blown and gotten stuck. Which is pretty much what it looked like before, to be honest.

If you're pursuing a more eclectic gallery wall, it's ideal if you can find pieces of varying sizes and orientations to really make your gallery wall sing. Start with a focal point—a primary larger piece, and then fill in with additional pieces that run horizontally, vertically, small-medium-weird shaped. All of this variety can add charisma to your gallery wall.

If you're aiming for something a little more modern, consider stream-lined frames in just a few sizes, all the same finish. This will help quiet the varied contents so that your gallery wall feels contemporary and clean, but also personalized.

For hanging: Let's be clear. Hanging a gallery wall is a bitch. It will require a good amount of forethought, a significant amount of measuring, and/or a laissez-faire attitude and a little spackle in the case of emergencies.

I highly recommend laying out your gallery wall on the floor first, and then taking detailed photographs of your layout before you start hanging. Aim to make the spacing between each relatively equal. Depending on how anal you are, you can drive yourself bonkers with this, or eyeball it, as you wish.

The size of your pieces will likely dictate the spacing between each of your pieces. If your collection is predominantly large format, you'll probably want at least 3"–4" between each piece. If it's a range of sizes, I wouldn't do much more than that between each piece. The idea is to give each piece a little space to breathe, without leaving it so far from the other pieces that it seems like you:

A. Didn't have enough art to fill your wall.
B. Are really bad at hanging art.
C. Forgot about that piece and then added it at the last minute.

About orientation:
Again, this is slightly specific to the style of gallery wall you're designing. If you're going with a more contemporary, tidy gallery wall, your frames may all be relatively similar, and that will limit your play with orientation.

However, if you're going for a more eclectic aesthetic (that's what we're calling your boyfriend's collection of bar coasters from every state and the onion horoscopes he's cut out for the last decade) then you've got a little more wiggle room with the direction and layout of your gallery wall. I'd still start by choosing a primary piece, and hanging that fairly off-center from the middle of your gallery space. This is because you don't want that main piece to look like the center of the sun, with all the smaller pieces radiating off of it like cheery little sun beams (God forbid). So by placing your largest piece off center, you can then stack two medium sized pieces to the left or right of that piece, and collectively, those three pieces become your "center." From there, build out. Ideally, I'd place a piece running vertically to the right of the stacked horizontals, probably a little higher or lower than them, and then continue building out, adding varying sizes of big, medium and small; though no other "big" piece will be larger than that first big piece you hung, or your whole outfit will start to feel off-kilter.

Like I said, hanging a gallery wall is a bitch. And now that you've read the "How To," I'm sure you can see the benefits of laying it on the floor rather than just going full-speed into hanging without a plan.

*or you could try the "Don't be a cliché" tactic, and hand this chapter to the man in your life and tell him to seize the day. I guess it's a question of principle vs. the path of least resistance. And now you know what school I belong to.

How to make the most of your art: framing like a pro, paying like an amateur.

IKEA, IKEA, IKEA. I can't stress this enough. Target has some good options, your local arts and crafts store will likely have a solid selection, but if you've got an IKEA anywhere near you, that's your joint!

First: They've got a million different sizes of the same style frame, which makes unifying your gallery wall significantly easier.

Second: All of their frames comes with a decent looking matting. Do you know the primary difference between that crap plastic frame you used to have for your posters and something that looks professionally framed? Okay, quality is an obvious factor, but the biggest difference in my book is the matting. A matting makes your otherwise cheap art look like the frame actually fits the art work properly. Professional, even.

Third: Their frames are cheap. Like so cheap. And if you go there and think, "This is expensive," go get a quote for a professionally-made custom frame and then we can talk about expensive. You don't know from expensive until you get a custom frame.

Fourth: They will continue to carry this same line of frames until long after you're dead, which is great because you'll be able to continue to add to your art collection and gallery wall and not have to reframe everything when you want to swap out that f-ing onion article for an actual piece of art work. Granted, you won't be able to take advantage of this once you're dead, but until then, it's a major plus.

Replacing Your Door Knobs

Believe it or not, this can be a truly transformative (though moderately boring), fairly easy home improvement project. I'm not suggesting you change the door knobs in your rental-hovel if you've got high hopes that you'll be moving on to cleaner pastures twelve months from now. But if you're in it for the long haul—crap apartment in a great location; long term lease; first time home ownership . . . then this is absolutely a project worth doing. You may not have noticed how cruddy your door hardware is up until now, but now that you're looking—chances are good you'll discover those plastic-y, flimsy bright gold buggers are all over your apartment. For reasons unknown (most likely because they're the cheapest version) this feeble hardware is a favorite among slum lords and shitty real estate developers alike, and unlike cheap paint or hideously-shiny wood floors, the door handles don't get replaced every time a new tenant moves in, so not only are they poorly made and lousy quality, they're also probably

from the early nineties, and have been handled by hundreds of people since they were installed. The mechanisms are loose, the screws holding it in place are looser, and there's probably ten years of stray paint around the edge.

For about ten dollars a door, you can easily swap these out for something a little more . . . purposeful. I'm not saying install ninety-five-dollar glass-ball-brass-rosette handles that will knock your socks off. I'm like forty years from being able to afford a ninety-five-dollar door handle. But, you can buy a subtle improvement—an understated brushed steel that says "Nothing."

It doesn't sing "I'm in the money," but it also doesn't announce, "This is a bug-infested motel!" and that's just the kind of message (or lack thereof) that we're after for this project.

So—now you know "why," let's discuss "how:"

Start by removing one of your existing door handles. You should find that one side has a pair of screws which are keeping it attached to the door. Remove those screws, and then pull off the handles. Usually once you remove those first two screws, everything else comes off fairly easily. Now, presumably, you've got a fairly typical door handle situation, which means that once you've removed the handle, you'll be left with a hole going right the way through your door, and another hole that bisects the first one- going left-to-right toward the door frame.

My recommendation would be to take your removed door hardware to the hardware store, to make sure you're buying a replacement handle that will fit without requiring additional modification. Count the number of door handles you need before you leave, and make sure you take note of which handles should be locking and which ones will be "passage handles," which means turning, but not locking.

One word of advice: Before you buy dozens of door handles, take a moment to think back to the door handles you've noticed in the past. Hard to remember, right? That's because a "good door handle" doesn't need to make a strong impression. So when you're shopping for your new handles, I discourage you from gravitating to something that's "quirky" or "exciting." Unless you're ready to throw down some real money on this hardware, your best bet is choosing something understated and architectural rather than something that stands out. Think about it like this: if someone put the handle in your handle, would you say, "This feels sturdy and well made" or would you say, "Wow! I've never seen a handle like this." Save the kooky handle for the extravagant renovation you do on your townhouse when you're an idiosyncratic, but lovable millionaire in your fifties.

Now that you've picked your handle hardware, follow the instructions provided with the hardware and ba-da-bing! Repeat installation steps on ALL of your doors (closets included) to make a cohesive, modernized transformation throughout your home. This part is tedious, but if you think about how many times you're going to use those handles over the next year, or five years, or ten—suddenly it seems worth it.

How to Trick Your Space into Feeling Larger and Brighter

I know I'm a broken record on this one, but the *number one* most effective way to make your space feel brighter and larger is . . . Say it with me: Put your shit away! Nothing diminishes a sense of spaciousness like disorder. Nothing detracts from natural light and brightness like piles of junk, needlessly interrupting every sight line in your space. I can't emphasize this enough—**PUT YOUR SHIT AWAY**.

Okay. Now let's imagine that everything is shipshape. Everything in its place and a place for everything. You are the pinnacle of organization, but your apartment still feels dreary and airless. What to do?

First, let's focus on your lighting. And specifically your light bulbs. Assuming we're working with generic overhead light fixtures (see page 120 for instructions on how to swap out those monstrosities), my personal bulb preference is for a dimmable 100-watt "warm white" bulb. Dimmable so that when we're seeking ambiance we can lower it to a flattering 40 watts, but bright enough that you don't feel like your eyes are malfunctioning during the day. Let's couple this 100-watt light bulb overhead with a pair of accent lamps—you know best if you need table lamps (to be positioned on your end tables or dining room console) or if you need a standing floor lamp because you just don't have an appropriate place to put a table lamp. The idea here is that you want to be able make your room as bright as possible for those days when you want crisp clear lighting, but have the versatility to make the space feel more romantic when that's preferable. Having a dimmable overhead fixture and a couple of supplementary lights is a sure-fire way to make your space feel desirably bright when needed, without making it feel like an interrogation room when it's not.

Now that our lighting is doing its best to improve the situation, let's talk about a couple of other handy tricks to create a false sense of spaciousness and brightness:
- Big art
- Big mirrors
- Neutral spaces and neutral colors
- Scale-appropriate light fixtures
- Well-positioned window treatments

• **Big art can be a terrific way to make your space feel larger and more airy.** It attracts the eye to it by making a bold, exciting statement, and distracts from the less wonderful attributes of your space (a.k.a. a lack of natural light). Combine large artwork with wide expanses of open wall space to allow the big art to really pop and grab your attention. If you have low ceilings, don't try to ram big art over your sofa—instead let it occupy a wall where it can hang uninterrupted from floor to ceiling to give it the most dramatic effect. And don't think that just because art is big means it has to be expensive. You can pick up

a large blank canvas at your local art store and for about fifty dollars for the canvas and supplies, you can whip out some of your very own "Abstract Art." I'm not kidding. Just do an image search for "Abstract Art" on Google and take a crack at channeling your inner Rothko. I'm not saying it's going to end up being museum-worthy, but it's definitely going to be better than that dog-eared Pulp Fiction poster you had in college. And you don't have to tell anyone you painted it. Just say you found it at an antique store and that will give it instant credibility.

But if homemade art isn't in the cards, consider searching online or at your local architectural salvage yard for a big piece of architectural molding—even a couple of big windows make a bold, bright statement—and are another fun way to trick your space into feeling more airy than it really is. Art doesn't have to be art in the traditional sense of "painting in a frame." It can be sculptural, like a piece of architectural salvage; or a clustering of similar objects, like a collection of silver trays—heck! You can even hang a textile or a small area rug and call it a "wall hanging." The idea is to make a bold impact, and then allow the adjoining spaces to be a little more quiet.

• **Big mirrors.** Got to love them. They reflect the natural light you do have, they double the sense of space in the room—there's really nothing not to like, unless you really hate your own reflection. The same notes on Big Art apply to Big Mirrors. Basically there's no such thing as too big when it comes to mirrors. Absolutely put a huge over-scale mirror above a console or over your sofa, and you can even be more daring with mirrors than you would with art work. One example: run mirrors from floor to ceiling and wall to wall—and then put your sofa in front of it if you want. I'm not saying that this is an inexpensive OR subtle idea, but my point is that if you decorate thoughtfully with and around mirrors, pretty much anything goes. And just so we're clear: Don't think you've got to buy a nine-hundred-dollar mirror from Restoration Hardware to make this work. One of my favorite mirrors is a heavily framed mirror from IKEA, which I painted to look like it was part of the architecture of our apartment. The whole thing cost about eighty dollars and people comment on it every time they come in my home. Craigslist and your local architectural salvage supply can also be a terrific place to hunt for less expensive, more spectacular mirrors—and don't underestimate the impact of repainting the frame to make it more effective.

• **Neutral surfaces and neutral colors:** The general power of the neutral surface has already been discussed in depth, but when talking about improving a sense of light and spaciousness, the impact of neutral surfaces is resounding. There are two reasons for this. The first is obvious—that a less crowded, less cluttered space will feel more open—which I know I've already covered. But the second affect is that those neutral open spaces also allow your more dramatic moments to really pop! Your Big Art won't look as bold or spectacular if it's surrounded by dozens of other little pictures. Let it hang on a wall alone so it can really dazzle the viewer. Likewise, employing a couple of neutral surfaces (neutral carpet, neutral wall color) can have the same impact—it's like the Pilates of home design—it will lengthen and strengthen your space and allow your strategically chosen accents to shine rather than crouch. When you're designing for a smaller space, try and think about how each surface is going to flow into the next. Ideally, the majority of your surfaces will blend subtly from one material into the next, with moments of excitement to enliven rather than overwhelm the space. I know that might feel a little bland, and I know you hate it when I say stuff like this, but try to remember that "bare is brighter than busy." I know. It's so boring. But it's also undeniably true, so suck it up.

The same applies when we're talking about a color palette for smaller spaces. I know it's fun to paint wild, daring colors, but if what you're trying to do is improve a sense of brightness and airiness in a small, dim apartment, dark bold colors are not your friend. Consider lights and whites, and if you've got the stamina (and permission from your land lord) you could even consider painting your floors white, or another bright, light color that complements your walls. I know this also feels boring, but it accomplishes the same thing you achieve when you leave some of your walls bare—your walls, ceiling, and floors flow into each other and the definition of ceiling height and spaciousness becomes much more vague.

• **Choosing appropriate light fixtures to make your space feel brighter:** I've already talked about better light bulbs, and in a different chapter we talked about replacing those generic soulless light fixtures that look like boring nipples, but what I'm talking about here is choosing light fixtures that are appropriate in scale to the space—with the goal of maximizing your sense of brightness and spaciousness without making the space feel overwhelmed by the fixture. The key here is not hanging a light fixture too low. Having to duck another a light fixture, or worse, a ceiling fan, is a guaranteed way to decimate the sense of spaciousness in your home. I know it's disappointing because there are so many awesome and inexpensive pendant lights available (IKEA and Lowes both have awesome selections these days!) but reserve those to hang over your dining table or if you must, over your bed, but not dangling in the middle of your living room for everyone to walk around. That's awkward and ugly. And even if it doesn't actually prevent someone from walking underneath it, if it looks like it's too low from a distance, it's still too low. Hanging a fixture that's too big for your space will only emphasize the lack of height you've got in your apartment, so if you've got to resign yourself to flush-mount fixtures, do it, but don't try to trick yourself into believing something is working when it's clearly not.

• **Well-positioned window treatments:** How you hang your window treatments can also have a huge impact on the sense of light and space in your home. If you hang drapes or shades within the window opening, you're inherently blocking almost a third of your window with the drapes themselves, even when they're pulled open. If you can afford to, the optimal way to hang your drapes would be as close to the ceiling as possible, approximately 6" to the left and right sides of the window molding, so that your drapes, when they're pulled back, cover the side moldings of your windows, along with 6" of wall to the left and right of the window, but don't actually block any of the window itself. Hanging the drapes so close to the ceiling will draw the eye upward and elongate each of the windows so they look more gracious and grand. If you can't spend that much money on your window treatments, consider installing the hardware into the face of the window moldings instead of inside the window recess, and then install tie back hardware into the left and right window moldings to keep your drapes pulled back, allowing as much natural light in as possible, without breaking the bank.

Okay, now that we've covered these tricks, can you identify the common theme here? At the heart of all of these tips, I'm basically just saying over and over, "Open. Open. Open." Bright colors = open. No clutter = open. Neutral spaces = open. Window treatments high and wide = open. Well positioned light fixtures = open. Big mirrors and big art, surrounded by empty walls = open.

So yeah. The best way to maximize your space is to improve the sense of openness in every possible way.

What's the Trick?
Finding Time for These Projects (without Losing Your Job, Friends, or Family)

Seriously, how does one find time to work all day, pursue meaningful (or meaningless) sexual and platonic relationships, stay current with Game of Thrones, and still have time for home improvement? When you write it out, it seems almost impossible. And yet . . . I assure you it can be done. Don't be a whiner. I've got a three-year-old, a full-time job, a seemingly endless family-tree, a husband who's trying to open a restaurant, and a really old dog. If I can squeeze it in, you can too.

Balance is vital. And don't underestimate the power of multi-tasking. You're right. You can not be in a bar and repainting your kitchen cabinets simultaneously. But you can listen to a pod-cast while you're painting your cabinets and then have something mildly interesting to talk about the next time you're in a bar. Also, once you've painted your cabinets, that's done. It's not like going to the gym. You don't have to keep going in order to see the results. You just paint them, let them dry, and then move on with your life. That applies to like, three-quarters of these projects. Once they're done, they're done. Yes, I'd really like it if you made your bed every morning, but honestly, it takes like two minutes. I'm pretty sure those two minutes aren't standing between you and your dream career/dream partner/dream body. And like I mentioned earlier, the sooner you put these systems in place, the sooner you decide where your dishes are going, the faster it will be to keep your cabinets organized. If you wash your dishes when you use them, it actually takes you less time to wash them than it does if you let them pile up into a fetid, food-caked heap for a week. If you'd just washed that egg off on

Sunday, you wouldn't be using a chisel to get it off on Wednesday. If you just hung up your clothes or put them in the hamper when you took them off, you wouldn't need to devote twenty minutes to sorting through them and hanging them all up at once.

My point is these projects aren't about sacrificing something else in favor of doing them. In the long term, it's much more about time management than compromise. Granted, when you make that initial push, maybe you'll have to give the bar the skip, and spend a little less time fucking around on Facebook, but once it's done, then the world's your oyster again, and you can lean against your beautifully upholstered headboard, basking in the luxury of your well-appointed bed with all its euro shams and throw pillows, and troll Pinterest until you've forgotten whether you love or loathe everything.

What I'm trying to say is you can prioritize these projects. You don't have to do them all, and you definitely don't have to do them all back-to-back. You should still see your friends and go to work. You should still watch your favorite shows and make it to your best friend's birthday party. But every once in a while, you can say, "Instead of doing that, I'm finally going to paint over that hideous color in the kitchen." And feel empowered knowing that you know how to do that. You CAN do that. And if you encounter a gorgeous pendant light at a stoop sale, you'll feel confident knowing that you CAN replace the horrible fixture in your bathroom. You CAN do that. The point is to tackle the things that are really standing between you and a more serene life, and keep the other projects in your back pocket until you're ready. Put your shit away. Hang up your clothes, do your dishes, get frames for all your shitty push-pinned posters . . . And then see how you're feeling. You may feel motivated by your overwhelming sense of progress. Those first couple of steps will transform your home. But they might also light a fire under your ass to keep improving. They might inspire you to paint that room or buy bedside lamps for your bedroom. And from there, the sky is the limit. What I'm trying to explain is—don't psych yourself into immobility. Take this shit one day at a time, one step at a time, and you can transform your space into the kind of home you're relieved to come back to, not the kind you have to wade through to get to your bed. Because God knows, we pay a lot for the place we sleep—we might as well enjoy it.